PROMOTING AND INCENTIVIZING CYBERSECURITY BEST PRACTICES

HEARING

BEFORE THE

SUBCOMMITTEE ON CYBERSECURITY, INFRASTRUCTURE PROTECTION, AND SECURITY TECHNOLOGIES

OF THE

COMMITTEE ON HOMELAND SECURITY HOUSE OF REPRESENTATIVES

ONE HUNDRED FOURTEENTH CONGRESS

FIRST SESSION

JULY 28, 2015

Serial No. 114–29

Printed for the use of the Committee on Homeland Security

Available via the World Wide Web: http://www.gpo.gov/fdsys/

U.S. GOVERNMENT PUBLISHING OFFICE

97–918 PDF   WASHINGTON : 2016

For sale by the Superintendent of Documents, U.S. Government Publishing Office
Internet: bookstore.gpo.gov   Phone: toll free (866) 512–1800; DC area (202) 512–1800
Fax: (202) 512–2104   Mail: Stop IDCC, Washington, DC 20402–0001

COMMITTEE ON HOMELAND SECURITY

MICHAEL T. McCAUL, Texas, *Chairman*

LAMAR SMITH, Texas
PETER T. KING, New York
MIKE ROGERS, Alabama
CANDICE S. MILLER, Michigan, *Vice Chair*
JEFF DUNCAN, South Carolina
TOM MARINO, Pennsylvania
LOU BARLETTA, Pennsylvania
SCOTT PERRY, Pennsylvania
CURT CLAWSON, Florida
JOHN KATKO, New York
WILL HURD, Texas
EARL L. "BUDDY" CARTER, Georgia
MARK WALKER, North Carolina
BARRY LOUDERMILK, Georgia
MARTHA McSALLY, Arizona
JOHN RATCLIFFE, Texas
DANIEL M. DONOVAN, JR., New York

BENNIE G. THOMPSON, Mississippi
LORETTA SANCHEZ, California
SHEILA JACKSON LEE, Texas
JAMES R. LANGEVIN, Rhode Island
BRIAN HIGGINS, New York
CEDRIC L. RICHMOND, Louisiana
WILLIAM R. KEATING, Massachusetts
DONALD M. PAYNE, JR., New Jersey
FILEMON VELA, Texas
BONNIE WATSON COLEMAN, New Jersey
KATHLEEN M. RICE, New York
NORMA J. TORRES, California

BRENDAN P. SHIELDS, *Staff Director*
JOAN V. O'HARA, *General Counsel*
MICHAEL S. TWINCHEK, *Chief Clerk*
I. LANIER AVANT, *Minority Staff Director*

———

SUBCOMMITTEE ON CYBERSECURITY, INFRASTRUCTURE PROTECTION, AND SECURITY TECHNOLOGIES

JOHN RATCLIFFE, Texas, *Chairman*

PETER T. KING, New York
TOM MARINO, Pennsylvania
SCOTT PERRY, Pennsylvania
CURT CLAWSON, Florida
DANIEL M. DONOVAN, JR., New York
MICHAEL T. McCAUL, Texas *(ex officio)*

CEDRIC L. RICHMOND, Louisiana
LORETTA SANCHEZ, California
SHEILA JACKSON LEE, Texas
JAMES R. LANGEVIN, Rhode Island
BENNIE G. THOMPSON, Mississippi *(ex officio)*

BRETT DeWITT, *Subcommittee Staff Director*
DENNIS TERRY, *Subcommittee Clerk*
CHRISTOPHER SCHEPIS, *Minority Subcommittee Staff Director*

CONTENTS

Page

STATEMENTS

The Honorable John Ratcliffe, a Representative in Congress From the State of Texas, and Chairman, Subcommittee on Cybersecurity, Infrastructure Protection, and Security Technologies 1
The Honorable James R. Langevin, a Representative in Congress From the State of Rhode Island 3
The Honorable Cedric L. Richmond, a Representative in Congress From the State of Louisiana, and Ranking Member, Subcommittee on Cybersecurity, Infrastructure Protection, and Security Technologies:
Prepared Statement 4
The Honorable Bennie G. Thompson, a Representative in Congress From the State of Mississippi, and Ranking Member, Committee on Homeland Security:
Prepared Statement 6

WITNESSES

Mr. Brian E. Finch, Senior Fellow, Center for Cyber and Homeland Security, George Washington University:
Oral Statement 7
Prepared Statement 9
Mr. Raymond B. Biagini, Partner, Covington and Burling:
Oral Statement 15
Prepared Statement 17
Ms. Andrea M. Matwyshyn, Visiting Professor, Center for Information Technology Policy, Princeton University:
Oral Statement 22
Prepared Statement 23

FOR THE RECORD

The Honorable John Ratcliffe, a Representative in Congress From the State of Texas, and Chairman, Subcommittee on Cybersecurity, Infrastructure Protection, and Security Technologies:
Letter 3

PROMOTING AND INCENTIVIZING CYBERSECURITY BEST PRACTICES

Tuesday, July 28, 2015

U.S. House of Representatives,
Committee on Homeland Security,
Subcommittee on Cybersecurity, Infrastructure
Protection, and Security Technologies,
Washington, DC.

The subcommittee met, pursuant to call, at 2:20 p.m., in Room 311, Cannon House Office Building, Hon. John Ratcliffe [Chairman of the subcommittee] presiding.

Present: Representatives Ratcliffe, Perry, Donovan, and Langevin.

Also present: Representative Watson Coleman.

Mr. RATCLIFFE. The Subcommittee on Cybersecurity, Infrastructure Protection, and Security Technologies will come to order.

The subcommittee is meeting today to examine the potential benefits of expanding the Support Antiterrorism by Fostering Effective Technologies Act, referred to as the SAFETY Act, to clarify that on a voluntary basis cybersecurity products and services can be reviewed and certified to receive enhanced liability protections for large-scale cyber incidents.

Right now, our cyber defenses are weak, and, because addressing cybersecurity vulnerabilities is costly, we need to find ways to promote and incentivize investment in cybersecurity. We need to incentivize companies to have a robust cyber-risk management plan in place. Through this hearing, we want to hear from our expert witnesses if the SAFETY Act Office at the Department of Homeland Security could be leveraged to promote and incentivize cybersecurity best practices within its existing framework.

By way of history, the SAFETY Act was part of the Homeland Security Act of 2002 and is a voluntary program that currently provides incentives for the development and deployment of anti-terrorism technologies. The SAFETY Act ensures that the threat of costly litigation does not deter potential manufacturers or sellers of anti-terrorism technologies at both large and small companies from developing and putting into the marketplace products and services that could reduce the risk or mitigate the consequences of a large-scale terrorist event.

Companies qualify for the protections afforded by the SAFETY Act by demonstrating through an on-going basis that they have a comprehensive and agile risk management plan. Applicants to this voluntary program must submit to a rigorous and thorough vetting process at DHS' SAFETY Act Office in order to receive liability protections in the event of an act of terrorism.

Homeland security and National security challenges are constantly evolving, and the cybersecurity threat is currently growing. It is in that capacity that earlier this year we passed H.R. 1731, the National Cybersecurity Protection Advancement Act. The goal of that legislation, which passed the House with a bipartisan vote of 355 to 63 and is now awaiting Senate action, is to strengthen the sharing of cyber threat indicators to guard against criminal groups, hacktivists, or nation-state actors.

Separately, we have been meeting with stakeholders to find other ways to strengthen cybersecurity, including expanding the SAFETY Act for cyber purposes. Right now, the SAFETY Act can only be triggered by an act of terrorism. However, for cyber attacks, attribution is extremely difficult to determine. Regardless of whether the hacker was a terrorist, a nation-state, a cyber criminal, or hacktivist, the impact of a devastating cyber attack would be the same.

If there is something more that can be done to increase cybersecurity best practices overall and potentially reduce the likelihood of a large-scale cyber attack, this subcommittee is going to examine it. SAFETY Act coverage for cybersecurity will not solve all of our cybersecurity challenges, but it has the potential to make a significant improvement in our Nation's cyber defenses.

In the coming weeks, the Committee on Homeland Security will consider House-passed legislation from the 113th Congress that would amend the SAFETY Act to establish a, "qualifying cyber incident," threshold to trigger SAFETY Act liability protections for vetted cybersecurity technologies.

The very creation of the Department of Homeland Security stemmed from the attacks on September 11, 2001. While we must and will remain vigilant and do everything we can to prevent another devastating attack on Americans, we must also recognize that the threat landscape in this country is changing. Cyber space is, in many ways, the new frontier, and a cyber 9/11 is only a matter of time if we fail to strengthen our cyber defenses. So we need to ensure that we are doing everything possible to harden our defenses left of boom, as they say in military parlance.

This potential legislation has the potential to increase investments in the security and resilience of our Nation's critical infrastructure, including the power grids, air traffic control, and banking systems.

Much of our Nation's critical infrastructure is privately owned, and in the 21st Century there now exists an interconnectedness of physical security and cybersecurity. This means that someone sitting at a keyboard can now initiate a physical injury by issuing commands at an office building, an air traffic control system, or someone's automobile, resulting in loss of life, not just the theft of personal information from a database.

Many products and services weren't built with cybersecurity in mind. This is why we need to incentivize market-driven solutions to raise the bar on how we manage our cybersecurity risks. Fortunately, the United States is home to an ingenuous entrepreneurial culture, and the best high-tech companies in the world have developed products and services that can help improve the information security resilience of our critical infrastructure and for companies that improve our quality of life.

If amending the SAFETY Act to include qualifying cyber incidents would better safeguard our Nation and potentially prevent a cyber attack that could shut things down and bring commerce to a screeching halt, then we owe it to ourselves and our constituents to examine the potential benefits it could provide. This is especially true given the increasing importance of cybersecurity in the lives of every American.

At this time, I ask unanimous consent to insert into the record a letter from the American Gas Association, the Edison Electric Institute, and the National Rural Electric Cooperative Association in support of testimony submitted by Mr. Brian Finch on the need to clarify the SAFETY Act to ensure that significant cybersecurity incidents are clearly covered.

Without objection, so ordered.

[The information follows:]

LETTER SUBMITTED BY CHAIRMAN JOHN RATCLIFFE

JULY 28, 2015.

The Honorable John Ratcliffe,
Chairman, Subcommittee on Cybersecurity, Infrastructure Protection, and Security Technologies.
The Honorable Cedric Richmond,
Ranking Member, Subcommittee on Cybersecurity, Infrastructure Protection, and Security Technologies, Washington, DC 20515.

DEAR CHAIRMAN RATCLIFFE AND RANKING MEMBER RICHMOND: On behalf of the American Gas Association (AGA), the Edison Electric Institute (EEI), and the National Rural Electric Cooperative Association (NRECA) we are writing in support of testimony submitted by Brian Finch on the need to clarify the SAFETY Act to ensure that significant cybersecurity incidents are clearly covered under the programs liability protections.

The electric and gas utility industries take cybersecurity threats very seriously. Any statutory clarification would be beneficial if it helps to make more explicit that cyber attacks are covered by the SAFETY Act and that legal defenses will be available to those using its certified cybersecurity products or processes in the event of a significant cyber attack. Currently, the SAFETY Act provides that liability protections are available in the case of an "act of terrorism," which is usually interpreted to include a significant cyber attack. To eliminate any doubt, Congress should make clear that it intends for a significant cyber attack to be covered. This clarification would likely result in an increase in utilization of the program and adoption of its certified cybersecurity products or processes.

We appreciate the subcommittee's continued focus on this important issue. The changes Mr. Finch has suggested are important and we look forward to working with you as legislation to clarify the SAFETY Act moves forward.

AMERICAN GAS ASSOCIATION.
EDISON ELECTRIC INSTITUTE.
NATIONAL RURAL ELECTRIC COOPERATIVE ASSOCIATION.

Mr. RATCLIFFE. I am pleased to be joined today by my colleague from Rhode Island, Mr. Langevin, who is filling in for Ranking Member Richmond.

The Chair now recognizes the gentleman from Rhode Island for any statement that he may have.

Mr. LANGEVIN. Thank you, Mr. Chairman.

I, too, want to welcome our witnesses here today.

Before I begin, Mr. Chairman, I would like to ask unanimous consent that Mrs. Watson Coleman of New Jersey be allowed to participate in this hearing, although she is not a Member of the subcommittee.

Mr. RATCLIFFE. Without objection.

Mr. LANGEVIN. Thank you, Mr. Chairman.

Next, as you mention, the Ranking Member is traveling with the President right now, so I am sitting in. I would like to ask unanimous consent to submit his opening statement for the record.

Mr. RATCLIFFE. Without objection, so ordered.

[The statement of Ranking Member Richmond follows:]

STATEMENT OF RANKING MEMBER CEDRIC L. RICHMOND

JULY 28, 2015

Good afternoon Mr. Chairman and thank you for holding this hearing on cybersecurity best practices.

I want to thank Dr. Andrea Matwyshyn from Princeton who has traveled to testify for us today.

The Department of Homeland Security, Science and Technology Directorate, is responsible for operating the SAFETY Act through the Office of Safety Act Implementation, or the OSAI.

While we are going to hear testimony today about the process for companies interested in having cybersecurity technologies designated as qualified anti-terrorism technologies under the SAFETY Act, we are also going to discuss some of the features of the draft SAFETY Act legislation that Chairman McCaul has circulated to industry.

The SAFETY ACT provides Government-sponsored immunity from liability to products or services that have gone through examination by the Office of Safety Act Implementation, and then designated, or certified under the SAFETY Act.

Congress has provided this kind of liability protection since 2002 to encourage innovation in the development of products and technologies for the homeland security enterprise that would help protect us from the terrorist threats or terrorist events, but only when the Secretary has determined that a terror event has taken place.

It would seem to me that the large, prime contractors who already supply the Department of Defense would need little help in providing the Department of Homeland Security with the kinds of services they might need in the civilian threat arena.

But small businesses are the backbone of America's workforce and innovation, creating most of the jobs in America. A SAFETY Act designation or certification for a new innovative product can improve a smaller company's bottom line and help resolve their concerns about liability protections. That was the original intent of the Act in 2002.

We are all concerned about the ability of American businesses, large and small, to protect their data and networks in today's amplified cyber threat atmosphere.

The question before us is how to best encourage civilian businesses to make sure their cybersecurity efforts are state-of-the-art, and how does SAFETY Act liability protection play a key role in helping us achieve that goal, in the complex, multi-layered arena of cybersecurity?

I look forward to the testimony today Mr. Chairman, and I yield back.

Mr. LANGEVIN. Very good. Thank you, Mr. Chairman.

So let me begin by saying that, as co-chair of the Congressional Cybersecurity Caucus with Chairman McCaul, I fully agree that organizations, public and private, must do a better job adopting cybersecurity best practices, as the consequences of cyber attacks can be devastating. I certainly also associate myself with the remarks of the Chairman in his opening statement, as well.

It is also abundantly clear that network administrators are not currently employing best practices, given that over 80 percent of cyber attacks could be stopped with simple hygiene measures like patch deployment or the use of two-factor authentication.

I understand that some of our witnesses today and the Chairman believe that applying existing policy, the SAFETY Act, to this problem may help improve our Nation's cybersecurity posture. I have great respect for their point of view, and I certainly believe that incentives are an avenue that we should explore. However, I do think that there are a number of questions this committee should answer as part of our consideration.

First, I think we must ask ourselves what we see as the underlying purpose of the SAFETY Act. I have always viewed the legislation as having at its heart the incentivization of research, design, and development of new technologies. Today, new information security products are being released at a prodigious rate, raising questions of whether further SAFETY Act protections are necessary to spur innovation. While the shield offered under SAFETY Act certification designation can certainly also incent deployment of these new, novel technologies, we at the committee must determine whether the act is properly tailored to the problem that we are addressing.

Second, we must also look into the implementation of technologies certified under the SAFETY Act. Network security is incredibly complex, and users of security products can often make mistakes in configuration or interpretation of results. For example, in the Target breach, the company's security software alerted on the malware that eventually compromised the point-of-sale terminals; however, the alert was lost in a sea of other warnings. How limits of liability would apply in such cases is an important concern.

Finally, we must examine the SAFETY Act in the context of cybersecurity risk management writ large. I have consistently fought efforts in Congress to prescribe specific technology solutions, either legislative or regulatory. Information technology simply moves too fast a pace to be able to say that today's best solutions will be viable in 5 years, let alone even less than that. Instead, I have advocated adoption of risk management frameworks like NIST that help companies assess their level of cybersecurity risk and development processes to reduce that risk.

One of the best practices universally praised under such frameworks is resilience—the idea that a network should not rely on a single technology for protection. Part of the reason that data breaches last for more than 6 months, on average, is that companies prioritize perimeter security without a similar focus on detecting anomalies once the network has in fact been breached. So the committee must explore whether the use of the SAFETY Act in a cybersecurity context could inadvertently make networks less resilient.

There are other questions I have—for instance, the adequacy of the certification process—that I hope the committee will also explore.

Let me again thank the Chairman for convening this important hearing. I thank the witnesses for appearing, and I certainly look forward to their testimony.

Mr. Chairman, before I yield back, I would just ask unanimous consent that the statement of the Ranking Member of the full committee, Mr. Thompson, also be entered into the record.

Mr. RATCLIFFE. Without objection, so ordered.

[The statement of Ranking Member Thompson follows:]

STATEMENT OF RANKING MEMBER BENNIE G. THOMPSON

JULY 28, 2015

Good afternoon. I want to thank Chairman Ratcliffe for calling today's hearing on encouraging cybersecurity best practices, and I want to thank the witnesses for testifying here today.

I especially want to thank Dr. Andrea Matwyshyn from Princeton University who has come to share her expertise and experience with us.

Today, we will be discussing the prospect of amending the SAFETY Act law to promote certification of more cybersecurity technologies as qualified anti-terrorism technologies. Given that there is draft legislation circulating, prepared by the Majority to amend the SAFETY Act in this manner, this hearing is timely.

Today, under the SAFETY ACT, DHS provides immunity from liability to products or services that have been rigorously examined by the Office of Safety Act Implementation.

Congress directed DHS to establish this program to encourage innovation in the development of novel anti-terrorism technologies.

As I noted in a previous hearing several years ago on this matter, the Government does not charge a penny to perform exhaustive reviews of each company's product that applies for, and is qualified for, SAFETY Act approval.

Mr. Chairman, I am wondering whether in our current fiscal situation, Congress should consider requesting a fee from companies with the means to seek pursue this process and desire to secure the liability protection and marketing advantage that comes with SAFETY Act certification.

When this committee first began to examine the activities of the SAFETY Act Office, I encouraged the Department to perform dedicated outreach to attract small, minority, and disadvantaged businesses to obtain SAFETY Act certification, and to help them go through the complicated and time-consuming SAFETY Act approval process.

The reasoning behind this emphasis was simple. Large multinational companies who are likely the prime developers of technologies in the homeland security enterprise, are mostly already involved with providing the Department of Defense technologies and services in that sphere.

In contrast, small businesses with promising technologies face countless barriers to entry in the marketplace. Given that these firms are often the innovators and the backbone of America's workforce, it is important that DHS go the extra mile.

A SAFETY Act designation or certification can improve a company's bottom line and help small, savvy companies create jobs. Large, well-funded companies need less help, and those companies are usually stocked with a bevy of corporate lawyers to guide them through any concerns about liability protections or access to DHS acquisitions.

The draft legislation that is in circulation has no special emphasis on small businesses. I am hopeful that as the bill moves through the legislative process, we can come together to ensure that it does.

I would also put on the record my concern that that the funding to expand the Safety Act Office would not be "new money" but rather taken from other DHS activities. It is important to know where that money would be taken from and what capabilities or programs would be affected or diminished.

More broadly, there are basic questions about how this legislation would drive innovation with respect to cyber technologies.

We would not want to foster an environment in the marketplace where companies grow complacent having only an interest in securing blanket liability protections outweighing the energy of innovation.

I look forward to the testimony today Mr. Chairman, and I yield back.

Mr. RATCLIFFE. Other Members of the committee are reminded that opening statements may be submitted for the record.

We are pleased today to have with us a very distinguished panel of witnesses on a very important topic.

Mr. Brian Finch is a senior fellow at the Center for Cyber and Homeland Security at George Washington University. Mr. Finch has a diverse background in homeland security issues and the SAFETY Act.

Thank you for being here, Mr. Finch.

Mr. Raymond Biagini is a partner at Covington and Burling. He has extensive experience and background in drafting the original SAFETY Act language and also assists companies in obtaining SAFETY Act certifications.

Welcome, Mr. Biagini.

Finally, we are pleased to be joined by Professor Andrea Matwyshyn—did I pronounce that right?

Ms. MATWYSHYN. You did.

Mr. RATCLIFFE [continuing]. Matwyshyn, who is a visiting professor at the Center for Information Technology Policy at Princeton University.

Professor, thank you for being here.

I would now ask each of the witnesses to stand and raise your right hands so I can swear you in to testify.

Do each of you swear or affirm that the testimony which you will give today will be the truth, the whole truth, and nothing but the truth, so help you God?

Let the record reflect that the witnesses have answered in the affirmative.

You may be seated.

The witnesses' full statements will appear in the record.

The Chair now recognizes Mr. Finch for 5 minutes for his opening statement.

STATEMENT OF BRIAN E. FINCH, SENIOR FELLOW, CENTER FOR CYBER AND HOMELAND SECURITY, GEORGE WASHINGTON UNIVERSITY

Mr. FINCH. Chairman Ratcliffe, Ranking Member Richmond, Mr. Langevin, distinguished Members of the subcommittee, my name is Brian Finch, and thank you for inviting me to testify before you today on how to effectively promote and incentivize cybersecurity best practices.

I firmly believe that promoting and incentivizing the use of cybersecurity best practices is critical to our Nation's security. The challenge, however, is determining what is, "the best," or even, "quite good." The SAFETY Act can help us with that right now.

Let me begin by stating what I will not be promoting in my testimony. I will not advocate for expanding the liability protections offered by the SAFETY Act or what triggers those protections. I will not seek to reinterpret the original intent behind the SAFETY Act. Rather, I will discuss how cyber attacks and cybersecurity technologies are covered under the SAFETY Act as currently written. I will also cover how a minor tweak to the law will improve its use in the cybersecurity context.

As this committee knows, SAFETY Act protections are triggered when the Secretary of Homeland Security declares that an, "act of terrorism" has occurred.

Under the SAFETY Act, an act of terrorism is defined as an event that is, "one, unlawful; two, causes harm to a person, property, or entity in the United States; and, three, uses or attempts to use instrumentalities, weapons, or other methods designed or intended to cause mass destruction, injury, or other loss to citizens or institutions of the United States." Nothing in that definition excludes cyber attacks.

Further, note that the SAFETY Act already explicitly states that cybersecurity technologies are eligible to receive liability protections. All of the above is why the DHS has already approved cybersecurity SAFETY Act applications.

Despite all of this, too many people are still unsure of whether the SAFETY Act applies to cyber attacks and cybersecurity technologies. To cure this, the House should once again unanimously pass section 202 of the National Cybersecurity and Critical Infrastructure Protection Act, or NCCIP. That section clarified the SAFETY Act by adding two new terms to it, "cyber incident" and "cybersecurity technologies." Those new terms merely made explicit protections already available under the SAFETY Act.

As we all know, the decision of Executive branch members to declare a particular event an act of terrorism in any context is a difficult one. Terms such as "workplace violence" and "cyber vandalism" are used instead of the "T" word. While I offer no opinions on the language used by the Executive branch to describe certain events, I can say that preventing or mitigating the outcomes that occurred in those events is exactly what Congress intended when it passed the SAFETY Act. That is why giving the Department of Homeland Security Secretary a term other than "terrorism" to use when bringing in the liability protections of the SAFETY Act is so important.

Now, if you will allow me, I would like to provide two examples where, if we could clarify the SAFETY Act, it would allow for vastly improved cybersecurity best practices.

First, let me talk about cyber risk groups. Companies could use risk-pooling mechanisms like risk-purchasing or risk-retention groups to increase their defenses and better mitigate risks.

Here's how that would work. First, a group of similarly-situated companies would agree to use certain security standards or technologies, such as, for instance, detonation chambers or the NIST Cyber Framework. Next, those companies would then either jointly purchase a cyber insurance policy or create a pool of insurance that they would all maintain and participate in. Third, the risk group would also agree to pursue SAFETY Act protections for the security standards that they have agreed to commit to adhering to.

All of this would be possible thanks to the vetting conducted under a clarified SAFETY Act. I would add that this pooling-risk purchasing agreement would be of particular value to small businesses, as well as to companies in historically underserved communities, as it would allow their dollars to travel further.

Next, cyber HMOs. I argue that cyber insurers should be using a health insurance model to promote best practices. Why? Because, under the cyber HMO model, it promotes wellness behavior that prevents minor scratches from developing into serious infections. That cyber HMO plan would also give the insured access to a vast network of cybersecurity vendors and professionals, as well as low-cost or free access to basic cyber hygiene, such as annual physicals, i.e., compromise assessments, or vaccines, in this case, perimeter defenses.

By encouraging the use of SAFETY Act-vetted products or services, the HMO and its policyholders would have greater confidence in the tools they are using to promote cyber health.

Thank you for the opportunity to testify, and I welcome any questions this committee may have.

[The prepared statement of Mr. Finch follows:]

PREPARED STATEMENT OF BRIAN E. FINCH

JULY 28, 2015

Chairman Ratcliffe, Ranking Member Richmond, distinguished Members of the subcommittee, thank you for inviting me to testify before you today on how to effectively promote and incentivize cybersecurity best practices.

My name is Brian Finch, and I am here today testifying in my capacity as a senior fellow with The George Washington University Center for Cyber and Homeland Security, where I am a member of the Center's Cybersecurity Task Force.[1] I am also a partner with the law firm of Pillsbury Winthrop Shaw Pittman LLP, a senior advisor to the Homeland Security and Defense Business Council, and a member of the National Center for Spectator Sport Safety and Security's Advisory Board.

Clearly, the implementation of best cybersecurity practices is critical to our Nation's economic security and physical safety. Our cyber enemies are numerous, growing, and increasingly sophisticated.

Fortunately there is no lack of will to defend ourselves from the attacks these enemies launch. Unfortunately, given the scale, scope, and pace of cyber threats we face, our cybersecurity measures writ large tend to lag behind the said attacks.

In light of those threats, I firmly believe that promoting and incentivizing the use of cybersecurity best practices and effective technologies, policies, and procedures are critical to our Nation's security. I also firmly believe that the private sector is ready and willing to adopt those best practices, technologies, policies, and procedures. Its challenge, however, is determining which of those items are in fact "the best" or even "quite good."

Moreover, we should all acknowledge that the private sector will see all of its cybersecurity decisions second-guessed in the tsunami of litigation that inevitably follows any cyber attack. Thus, programs that help companies determine which cybersecurity measures to adopt and will help them minimize their exposure to unnecessarily expensive and protracted litigation are desperately needed.

Thankfully, a program already exists in the United States Code that in fact does promote and incentivize the use of cybersecurity best practices, technologies, policies, and procedures: The "SAFETY Act."

The SAFETY Act, which stands for the Support Anti-Terrorism By Fostering Effective Technologies, was enacted in 2002 as part of the Homeland Security Act. The SAFETY Act is one of the most responsibly designed and effectively implemented liability management programs in Government today. More importantly, it can and already has been used to promote improved cybersecurity, and, with the leadership of this committee, that success can be expanded.

In my testimony below, I will go into greater detail as to how the SAFETY Act can currently be used promote the increased use of cybersecurity practices as well as effective technologies, procedures, and policies. I will also explain why I believe that some very minor statutory tweaks to the SAFETY Act would be exceptionally helpful in expanding its use in the private sector. Finally, I will also provide some examples of how the SAFETY Act could be tied to innovative ideas that will, in general, promote improved cybersecurity.

IMPORTANT CLARIFICATION REGARDING THE SCOPE OF THIS WRITTEN TESTIMONY

I believe at the outset that it is exceptionally important to establish what I will NOT be promoting in my testimony. I want there to be no misunderstanding with respect to what actions I believe Congress or the Executive branch should be undertaking in order to allow the SAFETY Act to reach its full potential with respect to cybersecurity.

Specifically, my testimony:
- Will NOT advocate for an expansion of the scope of the liability protections offered by the SAFETY Act. The SAFETY Act, as currently drafted, provides to the Department of Homeland Security (DHS) all of the legal authority needed to encourage the wide-spread deployment of effective and useful cybersecurity technologies, policies, and procedures;

---

[1] While I am testifying in my capacity as a senior fellow with The George Washington University Center for Cyber and Homeland Security, please note that my comments represent my personal views and not necessarily any positions of the Center.

- Will NOT advocate for an expansion of the types of unlawful events that may trigger the liability protections offered by the SAFETY Act. Again, as currently drafted, the SAFETY Act gives the Secretary of Homeland Security broad discretion to decide which unlawful acts that cause harm to U.S. persons, property, or economic interests can trigger its liability protections;
- Will NOT seek to revise or reinterpret the intent of the Members of the 107th Congress, who drafted and voted to enact the SAFETY Act;
- Will NOT advocate for the ability of the private sector to excuse itself completely from liability following a cyber attack, much less disincentivize the private sector from continually investing in and upgrading its cyber defenses; and
- Will NOT seek to undermine the ability of DHS to thoroughly review applications for SAFETY Act liability protections or require a dramatic expansion in the size or cost of the Office of SAFETY Act Implementation (OSAI), such that the program office will become unwieldy or unnecessarily costly.

Instead, my testimony will advocate for a very simple proposition: That with the addition of a few well-placed words, it will become perfectly clear to the private sector that the SAFETY Act applies to cybersecurity practices, technologies, procedures, and policies. Moreover, these minor tweaks will permanently clarify that the SAFETY Act applies to cyber attacks committed by a variety of actors, as well as attacks where attribution is unclear or impossible.

THE SAFETY ACT AS DRAFTED APPLIES TO CYBERSECURITY TECHNOLOGIES AND CYBER ATTACKS

A critical point that must be established immediately is that both the SAFETY Act statute (see 6 U.S.C. § 441–444) and the implementing Final Rule (see 6 CFR § 25) establish that cyber attacks can trigger the law's liability protections and that information technologies (including cybersecurity systems and services) are eligible to receive SAFETY Act liability protections. By way of review, please note that the SAFETY Act provides extensive liability protections to entities that are awarded either a "Designation" or a "Certification" as a Qualified Anti-Terrorism Technology (QATT). Under a "Designation" award, successful SAFETY Act applications are entitled to a variety of liability protections, including:

- All terrorism-related liability claims must be litigated in Federal court;
- Punitive damages and pre-judgment interest awards are barred;
- Compensatory damages are capped at an amount agreed to by both DHS and the applicant;
- That damage cap will be equal to a set amount of insurance the applicant must carry, and once that insurance cap is reached no further damages may be awarded in a given year;
- A bar on joint and several liability; and
- Damages awarded to plaintiffs will be offset by any collateral recoveries they receive (e.g., victims compensation funds, life insurance, etc.)

Should the applicant be awarded a "Certification" under the SAFETY Act for their QATT, all of the liability protections awarded under a "Designation" are available. In addition, the Seller of a QATT will be entitled to an immediate presumption of dismissal of all third-party liability claims arising out of, or related to, the act of terrorism.

The only way this presumption of immunity can be overcome is to demonstrate that the application contained information that was submitted through fraud or willful misconduct. Absent such a showing, the cyber attack-related claims against the defendant will be immediately dismissed.

Additionally, when a company buys or otherwise uses a QATT that has been either SAFETY Act "Designated" or "Certified," that customer is entitled to immediate dismissal of claims associated with the use of the approved technology or service and arising out of, related to, or resulting from a declared act of terrorism.

As the SAFETY Act is currently drafted, in order for its protections to be triggered, the Secretary of Homeland Security must declare that an "act of terrorism" has occurred. The definition of an "act of terrorism" is extremely broad and includes any act that:

    (i) is unlawful;

    (ii) causes harm to a person, property, or entity, in the United States, or in the case of a domestic United States air carrier or a United States-flag vessel (or a vessel based principally in the United States on which United States income tax is paid and whose insurance coverage is subject to regulation in the United States), in or outside the United States; and

(iii) uses or attempts to use instrumentalities, weapons, or other methods designed or intended to cause mass destruction, injury, or other loss to citizens or institutions of the United States.

The Secretary has broad discretion to declare that an event is an "act of terrorism," and once that has been declared, the SAFETY Act statutory protections will be available to the Seller of the QATT and others.

Critically, nothing in the SAFETY Act statute or Final Rule requires that there be a finding of a "terrorist" intent in order for the Secretary to declare that an "act of terrorism" occurred. Indeed, the only discussion of "intent" when defining an "act of terrorism" comes in the third part. There, all Congress drafted was that the attack must have used a weapon or other instrumentality "intended" to cause some form of injury.

Congress had every opportunity to explicitly or implicitly limit qualifying "acts of terrorism" to politically, religiously, or other ideologically motivated actions by specifically-defined groups or persons. It chose not to do so, instead stating that, for purposes of the SAFETY Act, an "act of terrorism" was simply an intentional unlawful act intended to cause harm to U.S. persons, property, or economic interests.

It can only follow then that the SAFETY Act statute can (and is) interpreted to include cyber attacks as an act that can be considered an "act of terrorism" and may serve as a trigger for the protections of the SAFETY Act.

Further, it is vital to note that the SAFETY Act Final Rule includes cybersecurity products and services in its definition of "Qualified Anti-Terrorism Technologies," or "QATT," or technologies that are eligible to receive SAFETY Act protections.

This point is readily demonstrated by the fact that DHS, through its Office of SAFETY Act Implementation, has already approved a number of cybersecurity products and services. By that measure alone, we know that the SAFETY Act applies to a variety of cybersecurity products and services.

Still, it is important to understand the statutory and regulatory basis for the coverage of cybersecurity products and services under the SAFETY Act.

We can start with the SAFETY Act itself, specifically in 6 USC § 444(1), defines a "Qualified anti-terrorism technology" as follows:

"For purposes of this part, the term "qualified anti-terrorism technology" means any product, equipment, service (including support services), device, or technology (**including information technology**) designed, developed, modified, or procured for the specific purpose of preventing, detecting, identifying, or deterring acts of terrorism or limiting the harm such acts might otherwise cause, that is designated as such by the Secretary." (emphasis added).

Note that this definition specifically covers "information technology" and, further, that the only characteristic needed by any product, equipment, service, device, or technology in order to be considered as a QATT is that the item "is designed, developed, modified, or procured for the specific purpose of preventing, detecting, identifying, or deterring acts of terrorism or limiting the harm such acts might otherwise cause."

Thus, by its explicit terms, information technologies—a term that includes cybersecurity products and services—are eligible to be considered as a QATT under the SAFETY Act.

We should also consider the QATT definition set forth in 6 CFR Part 25.2, which reads as follows:

"Qualified Anti-Terrorism Technology or QATT—The term 'Qualified Anti-Terrorism Technology' or 'QATT' means any Technology (**including information technology**) designed, developed, modified, procured, or sold for the purpose of preventing, detecting, identifying, or deterring acts of terrorism or limiting the harm such acts might otherwise cause, for which a Designation has been issued pursuant to this part." (emphasis added).

DHS also explicitly refers to information technologies when defining Qualified Anti-Terrorism Technologies and also links "information technologies" to any Technology designed, etc. to combat an "act of terrorism."

Therefore, any Technology designed, developed, modified, procured, or sold for the purpose of preventing, detecting, identifying, or deterring "acts of terrorism" will be eligible to be defined as a QATT. That includes cybersecurity products and services.

I would also refer the committee to the SAFETY Act Final Rule's definition of "Technology," which is as follows:

"Technology—The term 'Technology' means any product, equipment, service (including support services), device, or technology (**including information technology**) or any combination of the foregoing. Design services, consulting services, engineer-

ing services, software development services, software integration services, threat assessments, vulnerability studies, and other analyses relevant to homeland security may be deemed a Technology under this part." (emphasis added).

Please note that here again DHS specifically used the term "information technology," once again establishing that cybersecurity products, equipment, or services will be considered a "Technology" for purposes of the SAFETY Act.

Please note too that when elaborating on the types of "design services" that may be considered a "Technology" (a definition that includes various types of software development and support services), DHS stated that "analyses relevant to homeland security may be deemed a Technology under this part." See 26 CFR Part 25.2.

The use of the general term "homeland security" is of great import to this hearing. As this committee is well aware, DHS's "homeland security" mission is an "all hazards" one, which includes protecting against cyber threats in all forms. Indeed, in recent years the cybersecurity mission—whether related to terrorist groups, nation-states, organized crime, individuals, or others—has become a primary mission area for DHS. It follows then that when DHS defined "Technologies" for SAFETY Act purposes to include software services related to "homeland security," it intended that term to encompass cyber attacks in their myriad forms.

In summary, then, there is no question that cyber attacks, regardless of who conducted them or why, and cybersecurity products and services are eligible to receive SAFETY Act protections under the plain language of the SAFETY Act statute and the Final Rule as originally drafted.

THE NATION WOULD BENEFIT IF CONGRESS WERE TO AMEND THE SAFETY ACT IN A WAY THAT MAKES ITS COVERAGE OF CYBER ATTACKS CYBERSECURITY TECHNOLOGIES EVEN MORE EXPLICIT

Despite the fact that the SAFETY Act, as already drafted, encompasses both cybersecurity products and services and cyber attacks unconnected to specific "terrorist" groups or motivations, too many people are unsure of whether the SAFETY Act applies to exactly those items and situations. In short, the only way to rectify the situation is for Congress to slightly amend the SAFETY Act to make explicit its coverage of cyber attacks and cybersecurity products and services.

Thankfully, the path and process for clearing up the SAFETY Act's application in the cyber context has already been blazed, and all this committee and the House of Representatives need to do is retrace its steps.

In the 113th Congress, Members of this committee, including Chairman McCaul, Ranking Member Thompson, Representative Meehan, and Representative Clarke introduced the National Cybersecurity and Critical Infrastructure Protection Act (NCCIP).

Section 202 of the NCCIP would have slightly altered the SAFETY Act by essentially adding two new terms to the existing law: "Cyber incident" and "cybersecurity technologies." These new terms would be inserted after the words "act of terrorism" and "anti-terrorism technologies," respectively, in the existing SAFETY Act law.

The purpose of these new terms was simple and straightforward: Make it 100% clear to potential users of the SAFETY Act that the law applies to cybersecurity products and services as well as to cyber attacks that one might not colloquially put in the same category as the terrible events of Sept. 11, 2001 or the Boston Marathon bombings.

These changes were apparently not controversial to this committee or this Chamber, as H.R. 3696 passed the House by unanimous voice vote. Unfortunately, due to timing issues that prevented the resolution of some concerns by a few Senators, Section 202 was not included when the final version of H.R. 3696 passed the Senate and was signed into law. Still, I remind this committee again that Section 202 was passed unanimously by the House, and so this committee should pass the SAFETY Act clarifying language once again.

This clarification continues to be absolutely vital for a variety of reasons. First, I can state without qualification to this committee that the vast majority of eligible SAFETY Act applicants do not realize after reading its statutory language that the SAFETY Act covers non-"terrorist"-related cyber attacks or even cybersecurity products and services in general.

Rather, most people who are not steeped in the nuances and history of the SAFETY Act simply see the words "act of terrorism" and "Qualified Anti-Terrorism Technologies" and think only in terms of al-Qaeda, ISIS, right-wing militias, and the like.

The statute or Final Rule evidences no such limitations, and, further, there is no legislative history that I am aware of that would definitively limit the application of the SAFETY Act to such groups, their actions, or items designed to deter, defeat, or combat them.

Inclusion of Section 202 language would eliminate that confusion. All parties would now be fully on notice of the application of the SAFETY Act to cyber incidents and cybersecurity technologies, thus allowing everyone to get on to the business of deciding whether the SAFETY Act is right for them or if the product or service merits the liability protections it offers.

Second, inserting the term "cyber incident" would be of great value to the Executive branch, particularly the Secretary of Homeland Security. Under the SAFETY Act, the decision to declare an incident an "act of terrorism" is assigned to the Secretary of Homeland Security. Thus she or he is the person who decides whether a company that holds a SAFETY Act award may actually assert the defense in Federal court. Without that designation, the defenses of the SAFETY Act are not available under the law to the SAFETY Act awardee.

As the past few years have demonstrated, the decision of Executive branch members to declare a particular event an act of terrorism in any context is a difficult one. From the shootings at Fort Hood to the cyber attack on Sony Pictures, and even to the recent cyber attack on the U.S. Office of Personnel Management, the Executive branch treads very cautiously when deciding how to describe an incident. Creative terms such as "workplace violence", "cyber vandalism", or even references to a general "security breach" are used instead of the "T" word.

I offer no opinions on the terms used by the Executive branch in those incidents, yet I would dare say we all agree that there is no disagreement on their impact on American lives and our economy. Lives were lost, businesses were crippled, and Government programs have been crippled for years to come. It is those outcomes—or more specifically preventing or mitigating them—that Congress was focused on when it passed the SAFETY Act in 2002.

That is why adding the term "cyber incident" as defined in Section 202 of NCCIP is a vital tool to give to the Homeland Security Secretary. The Secretary should have the same flexibility to acknowledge the seriousness of a given incident, and, in the case of the SAFETY Act, trigger specific liability protections, without having to utilize a term that may cause a larger than necessary impact. Section 202 thus represents a simple tool with which to wield the SAFETY Act with greater delicacy.

Finally, I must emphasize that the language of Section 202 only clarifies the SAFETY Act and is entirely consistent with the original intent of the law. Section 202 does not expand the SAFETY Act, as have argued.

When one looks back at the creation, implementation, and use of the SAFETY Act, it has always been clear that the purpose of the law has been to promote the use by the private sector of useful and effective security products and services in order to deter or mitigate massively damaging unlawful events.

The SAFETY Act was designed to help mitigate those events by providing the possibility of limited liability protections following the unlawful "act of terrorism." These liability protections were deemed needed because of concerns about potentially endless litigation following a major attack.

Time has borne out those concerns. The attacks of 9/11 spurred litigation that lasted more than a decade and whose costs ran well into the hundreds of millions of dollars. Similar litigation arising out of the 1993 World Trade Center attack also lasted for more than a decade, and now every new terrorist incident spurs numerous new lawsuits.

Cyber attacks are no different. High-profile attacks spur multiple lawsuits, and indeed the cost of managing litigation post-cyber attack is beginning to represent one of the most expensive consequences of a cyber attack. Considering that millions of cyber attacks occur daily, and that these attacks are growing more sophisticated and successful with each passing moment, liability protections for cybersecurity vendors and users are absolutely critical.

This is especially true given that many of these attacks are conducted by foreign governments and are essentially unstoppable by the private sector. That fact will not deter plaintiffs' counsel, however, and so no matter how good a product is or how much is invested in defensive programs, companies will still face massive litigation. That trend cannot continue, and so it is only proper to use the SAFETY Act as originally intended to control that outrageous trend.

In summary then, clarifying—but not amending—the SAFETY Act so that it explicitly covers cyber incidents and cybersecurity technologies is not only appropriate given the seriousness of the cyber threat. It is also appropriate given the general misunderstanding of how the SAFETY Act works and the need to provide flexibility to the Homeland Security Secretary when determining whether to let the protections of the SAFETY Act be applied.

OPTIMIZING USE OF A CLARIFIED SAFETY ACT

Clarifying the SAFETY Act so that it clearly applies to non-"terrorist" cyber attacks and cybersecurity products and services will have multiple benefits. Please allow me to highlight two examples of improved cybersecurity this committee would likely support that would benefit from a clarified SAFETY Act.

(1) "Cyber Risk Groups"

One challenge facing private-sector companies when implementing cyber defenses is how to effectively cooperate with other companies to protect themselves and best use their limited resources. Particularly using a clarified SAFETY Act, companies could use risk-pooling mechanisms to increase their defenses and better mitigate risk.

Risk-pooling mechanisms come in a number of forms, including "risk purchasing" and "risk retention" groups. Those groups allow collections of companies (usually similarly situated in terms of industry sector) to jointly purchase or create insurance coverage that would otherwise be unavailable or excessively expensive.

Here's how it can work:

1. A group of similarly-situated companies agree to form a risk purchasing or retention group in order to obtain cybersecurity insurance.

2. The companies agree to use certain security standards or technologies (for instance SANS 20 controls, "detonation chambers," information sharing via dedicated "private clouds," the recent National Institutes of Standards and Technologies voluntary cybersecurity framework, etc.)

3. The companies then pool their resources to either jointly purchase an existing cyber insurance policy or to create a pool of insurance that they would maintain.

4. The risk group also agrees to pursue SAFETY Act protections for the standards it has created and committed to adhering to.

5. As part of the agreement, any company that fails to adhere to the security standards will be asked to leave the group at the next renewal period.

Using a clarified SAFETY Act on top of the insurance pool effectively limits the exposure of the group to the amount of insurance they have purchased, or even a portion thereof.

Further, this arrangement also potentially allows more of the insurance funds to be used for losses the company has directly suffered (damaged equipment, lost data, business interruption, etc.) rather than losses suffered by third parties.

The pool arrangement allows companies to collaborate and establish a baseline of security that each would commit to maintaining, all of which fall under the umbrella of a review by DHS. None of this would be possible without a clarified SAFETY Act.

I would add the pooling/risk purchasing agreement would be of particular value to small businesses or ones that serve historically underserved communities. For instance, cooperatives that provide utility services would benefit greatly from this arrangement as it would allow them to provide broader cybersecurity at reasonable costs to their members. Considering that their members are in historically underserved communities, this would be an excellent public benefit every member of this committee could support.

(2) "Cyber HMOs"

A challenge this committee and others have faced is how to use cyber insurance to promote best cybersecurity practices. That problem remains unsolved, but I contend a clarified SAFETY Act can help the Nation better utilize insurance solutions.

First, I start with the proposition that cyber attacks are a constant threat, much more akin to medical claims than property or casualty claims. We know they will occur on a regular basis, and so insurers need to establish an infrastructure that supports constant care over a lifetime.

Following on the health care analogy, cyber insurers should view their policies through the lens of a health insurance model and not a general liability or casualty policy. In my mind, it follows then that cyber insurers should develop cyber policies using a "HMO" model.

Under that model, the insurer's goal will be to promote the "right" kinds of claims—ones that encourage healthy behavior. Yet even with the incentivizing of healthy behavior, inevitably some sort of disease will work its way into the blood stream. The cyber HMO model works well here too as it will support interventional care that prevents minor scratches from developing into a serious infection.

A best-case scenario would work out this way: A "cyber HMO" is established, which companies can gain access to by paying monthly premiums along with associated "co-pays," "deductibles," and similar expenses typically associated with a health insurance plan.

That cyber HMO plan would give the insured access to a vast network of cybersecurity vendors and professionals at discounted rates that could be called upon in the event of a problem (the "co-pays" and "co-insurance" equivalents).

The cyber HMO plans would also provide low-cost or even free access to basic "cyber hygiene" care, such routine diagnostic examination of information technology systems, perimeter defense systems, and other basic defense systems (the "annual physical" and "low-cost or free vaccine" equivalents).

More "advanced" defense systems could be subject to a higher co-pay and deductible, and companies could even chose to go "out of network" if they want, but they would have to shoulder more of the cost.

The clarified SAFETY Act would help here, too, by helping decide whether a cybersecurity product or service should be "covered" under this insurance model. By encouraging the use of products or services vetted by DHS through the SAFETY Act, the HMO and its policyholders would have greater confidence in the tools they are using to promote cyber health.

The "cyber HMO" is one that actively rewards healthy cyber behavior—a Gordian knot that no carrier has been able to untie yet using traditional insurance models. That's a critical piece of the cybersecurity puzzle, as the challenge has been how to get companies to engage in effective cybersecurity, rather than any form of cybersecurity.

CONCLUSION

Thank you for the opportunity to testify before the committee today. I will be happy to answer any questions you might have.

Mr. RATCLIFFE. Thank you, Mr. Finch.

The Chair now recognizes Mr. Biagini for 5 minutes for his opening statement.

STATEMENT OF RAYMOND B. BIAGINI, PARTNER, COVINGTON AND BURLING

Mr. BIAGINI. I thank you, Mr. Chairman. Thanks for having me here. I thank the Members of the committee for this opportunity. Indeed, it's a privilege to speak with you about the possible expansion of the SAFETY Act to cover qualifying cyber incidents.

Let me address in short what I see as the key questions for this committee's consideration.

First, are liability protections needed to incentivize companies to enhance their own cybersecurity systems and to incentivize providers of cyber solutions to design more effective technologies? I believe the answer is yes.

In short, we face a potentially devastating existential cybersecurity threat. As I outline in my written remarks, the magnitude of this threat cannot be overstated. The 9/11 Commission authors likened a cyber attack on U.S. critical infrastructure to the terrorist threat before September 11, calling the cyber domain as the battlefield of the future.

Those distinguished authors of the Commission report recommended legislation to incentivize the design and deployment of cybersecurity. We only have to look at the recent hack at OPM to confirm that the cyber wolf is knocking at our critical-infrastructure door.

There is also a sense that corporations are moving too slowly to upgrade and enhance their own cybersecurity within their corporate walls.

Regarding cyber insurance, carriers often lack the data they need to quantify losses from cyber attacks. When they do write cyber insurance, it often has large deductibles, inadequate limits, and exclusions for attacks by nation-states. This is particularly concerning for companies involved in cybersecurity in the critical infrastructure arenas of health care, financial, electrical, and energy.

The laudable efforts by NIST to get companies to participate in the basic cyber hygiene program may be progressing too slowly. So I believe the enormity of the risk, coupled with the slowness of corporations' self-policing, and with some softness in the insurance markets, a surgical, legislative, incentivizing solution is appropriate.

But the second question is: Why turn to the SAFETY Act as a vehicle to be used for this incentivizing approach?

I have had the fortunate experience over the past 13 years to not only witness but to play an active role in the significant evolution of the SAFETY Act, as itself a truly best practice among homeland security companies big and small. The SAFETY Act has, in fact, stimulated companies to do cutting-edge research, design, development, and deployment of anti-terror technology and to incur the end-users to buy and deploy SAFETY Act technologies.

From the very beginning of the act, small companies have benefited. The first recipient of SAFETY Act coverage was a small company, Michael Stapleton Associates, who got SAFETY Act coverage for their anti-terror training regimen for bomb-sniffing dogs.

Fast-forward to today. DHS is granting SAFETY Act coverage to the likes of the Port Authority of New York and New Jersey for a complement of highly sophisticated anti-terror technologies to protect the new Freedom Tower. They have provided SAFETY Act coverage to the Kentucky International Airport and its cybersecurity programs and to a small and growing number of cybersecurity companies providing vulnerability assessments and resiliency testing of cyber networks.

The SAFETY Act Office has shown that they can expedite coverage when deployments are subject to Federal contracts and give great weight to technologies that have preexisting positive track records in the Federal or military space.

In short, the SAFETY Act and its implementers have shown a demonstrable ability to evolve and address emerging technologies of increasing complexity. Properly resourced, I believe they can do so in the SAFETY Act if it is expanded through this amendment.

I want to mention that I know—that, indeed, the SAFETY Act is helping to improve the technology that is out there, and here is why. Every day, almost every week, I get approached by companies that would like to pursue SAFETY Act coverage, and many, many times I tell them they are not ready. They are not ready for SAFETY Act coverage at this time, because they don't have the bona fides yet. They may not have had sufficient testing done or self-evaluation of their technologies. They may not have done important hazards analysis or risk analysis. They may not have done the operational and training manuals that the SAFETY Act Office will require them to have.

Many, many times, those same applicants come back around about 2 months later or 3 months, and they have the bona fides, and they have improved their technology, and now they are ready to seek SAFETY Act coverage. So, in this sense, the SAFETY Act has, indeed, acted as a gatekeeper.

The last point I would like to make, Mr. Chairman, is that, as you mentioned, oftentimes the SAFETY Act—amending the SAFETY Act to cover cyber attacks. Cyber attacks cannot often be attributed to terrorists. It just makes sense to amend the SAFETY Act, because cyber attackers, by nature and often deliberately, do not leave behind the "whodunnit" signature that terrorists crave, in fact proclaim, after they commit a horrific attack. The amendment here properly focuses on the "what," did the cyber attack cause material damage severely affecting the United States, not on the "who," in terms of whether it was a terrorist or not.

I believe that the cause here is worthy, the circumstances are sufficiently compelling, and I believe the results will be salutary.

Thank you, Mr. Chairman.

[The prepared statement of Mr. Biagini follows:]

PREPARED STATEMENT OF RAYMOND B. BIAGINI

JULY 28, 2015

Good afternoon. Thank you, Chairman Ratcliffe, and the Members of this subcommittee, for the opportunity—indeed privilege—to speak with you today about this important topic of potentially expanding the U.S. SAFETY Act to provide needed liability protections arising out of "qualifying cyber incidents," as that term is described in the proposed amendment. I support the proposed approach.

I have a particularly keen interest in this topic, and note that I have always been hesitant to engage in activities that might lead to the amendment of the SAFETY Act, because I am the original author of the core liability protection provision of the SAFETY Act. I wrote that provision in June 2002 at the request of some of our law firm's homeland security contractor clients. Together, we examined the legal landscape and homeland security marketplace immediately following the horrific attacks of 9/11 and quickly recognized the need for new legislation to address key public policy needs:

- To stimulate companies, large and small, to research, design, develop, and deploy cutting-edge anti-terror technology without fear of enterprise-threatening liability suits.
- To stimulate the terror insurance market which had stopped providing terror coverage after the 9/11 attacks.
- To enhance homeland security in the United States and abroad.

Guided by these policy considerations, I drafted in June 2002 the "Certification" section (now Section 863(d)(1), (2), and (3)) of what became the U.S. SAFETY Act, passed by Congress in November 2002 as part of the Homeland Security Act. In short, the SAFETY Act is landmark legislation, eliminating or minimizing tort liability for sellers or providers of anti-terror technology ("ATT") approved by U.S. Department of Homeland Security ("DHS") should suits arise in the United States after an act of terrorism.

As described more fully below, DHS has awarded SAFETY Act coverage for hundreds of cutting-edge anti-terror products and services since its inception in 2002, thereby satisfying many of the policy concerns described above. In fact, in many respects, the SAFETY Act has become a homeland security industry "best practice" risk management technique, spurring companies, including small businesses, to research, design, develop, and deploy anti-terror technology to protect America without fear of "enterprise-threatening" tort liability should there be another 9/11 terror incident. But given the remarkably rapid expansion over the past several years of increasingly penetrating cyber attacks on key sections of the American economy and Government infrastructure, it is time to thoughtfully consider a surgical upgrade of the SAFETY Act so that that law can "catch up" to the realities of the cyber threat we now face. In short, the proposed legislation recognizes a fundamental principle: The "trigger" of liability protections for a "qualifying cyber attack" should turn not on the identity of the attacker, i.e., is he or she a terrorist, but on the severity of the attack on critical U.S. interests. Moreover, this amendment will begin to requite the public policy concerns that existed in 2002 and exist today—the need to incentivize companies to further develop cutting-edge cyber solutions and to upgrade and enhance their cybersecurity systems; and the need to stimulate the availability of cyber insurance, particularly for key high-value cyber targets in the energy, aviation, electrical, and health care industries. These public policy and marketplace dynamics auger for thoughtful consideration of this proposed legislation.

A. KEY FEATURES OF THE SAFETY ACT

1. Liability Protections

Should a company obtain SAFETY Act tort protection from DHS, these protections fall into one of two categories:

"Certification—the highest form of protection—creates a presumption that the seller of ATT is immediately dismissed from suit unless clear and convincing evidence exists that the seller acted fraudulently or with willful misconduct in submitting data to DHS during the application process. Certification coverage also eliminates punitive damages claims; requires that any suit after an act of terrorism be filed in Federal court; and caps the awardee's liability, usually at its terror insurance limits."

Certification coverage is usually awarded by DHS when the applicant's technology has been widely deployed and has a track record of "proven effectiveness."

The lesser form of SAFETY Act coverage is known as "Designation" coverage and is usually provided when the anti-terror technology has limited actual deployment in the field:

"Designation—provides all of the protections under Certification coverage except the presumption of dismissal."

Importantly, certification and designation protections apply "up and down" the supply chain, i.e., the awardee's subcontractors, vendors, and distributors "derivatively" obtain the same SAFETY Act tort protections as the awardee. But most important, those that buy or deploy SAFETY Act-approved technology—whether they are commercial or Government customers—also are protected derivatively from tort liability arising out of an act of terror.

2. Limits on the Liability Protections

The SAFETY Act's liability protections are triggered only if DHS's Secretary designates a particular incident an "act of terrorism" under the SAFETY Act. "Act of terrorism" is defined as an unlawful act causing harm to a person, property, or entity in the United States, using or attempting to use instrumentalities, weapons, or other methods designed or intended to cause mass destruction, injury or other loss to citizens or instrumentalities of the United States. The Secretary of DHS will determine on a case-by-case basis whether a particular terrorist attack is covered under the SAFETY Act. This threshold statutory requirement to first designate a particular attack as an "act of terrorism" under the SAFETY Act before the liability protections are applicable is an obvious limitation that may not be necessary or appropriated in considering whether to expand the SAFETY Act to "qualifying cyber incidents."

The SAFETY Act can also apply "extraterritorially," i.e., even if the act of terror occurs outside the United States, the SAFETY Act can apply to suits filed in the United States so long as the "harm," to include financial harm, is suffered by U.S. persons, property, instrumentalities, or entities. And SAFETY Act protections can also apply "retroactively" to cover anti-terror technologies that an applicant has already deployed and which are substantially equivalent to those technologies for which it has obtained coverage.

The SAFETY Act defines "loss" as death, injury, or property damage, including business interruption loss. The definition of "anti-terror technologies" includes "any product, equipment, service (including support services), device, or technology (including information technology)" which has a material anti-terror purpose.

Finally, in order to obtain the tort liability protections, an applicant for SAFETY Act coverage must carry terror insurance which will respond to third-party tort liability suits arising out of a covered act of terrorism. The cost of the insurance cannot unreasonably distort the pricing of the anti-terror technology. The terror coverage limits usually become the applicant's ultimate "cap" on liability. In practice, if an applicant does not have terror coverage, the SAFETY Act Office will work with the applicant to find terror coverage at a price that the applicant can afford.

B. THE SAFETY ACT AS IMPLEMENTED SINCE 2002

Over the past 13 years, particularly in the last 7–8 years, DHS has vigorously implemented the SAFETY Act, providing coverage to hundreds of companies—from small businesses to some of the largest corporations in the world—for the anti-terror products or services they provide in the United States and abroad. In fact, the first

SAFETY Act award went to a small company, Michael Stapleton Associates, for its bomb-sniffing dog training regimen, its X-ray screening, and bomb detection system.

Representative SAFETY Act awards over the past 13 years include coverage for:
- threat and vulnerability assessment protocols;
- airport baggage handling systems;
- biometrically-secured airport identification and access system under the Registered Traveler Program;
- perimeter intrusion detection systems;
- cargo inspection systems deployed at ports and borders;
- physical security guard services;
- secure broadband wireless communications infrastructure and command-and-control systems;
- lamp-based infrared countermeasure missile-jamming systems;
- anti-IED jamming systems.

In some of these cases, the SAFETY Act Office was able to "expedite" its review and award of coverage by giving weight to the fact that these anti-terror products and services had proven effectiveness through long-term deployments with Federal and military customers.

Importantly, DHS has also awarded SAFETY Act coverage to private and quasi-Governmental entities for their security protocols, procedures, and policies used to determine the nature and scope of security they deploy to protect their own facilities and assets. Specifically,
- a major chemical company obtained coverage for its facility security services, including its vulnerability assessments, cybersecurity, emergency preparedness and response services, and its perimeter security, at its facilities that were governed by the Maritime Transportation Security Act;
- the Cincinnati/Northern Kentucky Airport obtained coverage for its security management plan, its operations and training procedures for its airport police, rescue, and firefighting personnel, its emergency operations center, and airport security plans;
- the New York/New Jersey Port Authority obtained coverage for the security assessments and design/architectural engineering services incorporating security-related design features at the New Freedom Tower and World Trade Center site;
- the NFL obtained coverage for the stadium security standards and compliance auditing program;
- three large professional sports venues obtained coverage for their security practices and protocols;
- the New York Stock Exchange Security System obtained coverage for its command-and-control and integration of a multi-layered security system.

These significant awards, as well as the fact that the Federal Acquisition Regulations now require Federal agencies issuing homeland security solicitations to first consult with the DHS SAFETY Act Office to determine if expedited coverage is appropriate, have helped the SAFETY Act toward reaching its full potential.

C. THE PROPOSED LEGISLATION: A LIMITED BUT APPROPRIATE EXPANSION OF THE SAFETY ACT TO COVER QUALIFIED CYBER INCIDENTS

1. Current Atmospheric Conditions

The cyber threat to U.S. Governmental institutions and critical infrastructure as well as to commercial entities is increasing at an alarming rate. Examples include:
- the recent hack into OPM affecting over 22 million individuals, apparently by China;
- the 2014 attack on J.P. Morgan involving cyber theft of data belonging to 76 million households, likely by Russia;
- the attack on Sony Pictures, apparently by North Korea;
- the indictment of 5 Chinese military officials for hacking proprietary data held by Westinghouse and U.S. Steel.

Indeed, on July 22, 2014, the 9/11 Commission authors likened the threat of a cyber attack on U.S. critical infrastructure to the terrorist threat before September 11, 2001, calling "the cyber domain as the battlefield of the future." These authors urged legislation to incentivize enhanced cybersecurity. Further, the United States has identified cyber attacks as the single greatest threat to National security and at the forefront of the Nation's defense and critical infrastructure, characterizing cyber attackers as undeterred by the threat "we'll shutdown your systems" if you attack ours.

In addition to these policy-level concerns, market dynamics are at work. Many companies are slow to improve their systems to prevent or mitigate against an attack. Cyber insurance for key sectors of the economy, especially critical infrastructure, e.g., health, financial, can be hard to get and expensive, often containing significant exclusions. The U.S. goal to strengthen cybersecurity resilience by having industry voluntarily follow NIST guidelines is progressing slowly. DHS, Commerce, and Executive branch agencies have suggested that tort mitigation legislation may be necessary to stimulate industry to enhance cybersecurity and the insurance industry to increase its footprint in the cyber market.

2. Why Amend the SAFETY Act to Cover Non-Terror-Based "Qualifying Cyber Incident?"

There are numerous reasons that a discriminate expansion of the SAFETY Act makes sense as a means to mitigate increasing cyber threats. The first has to do with the inherent characteristics and differences between a cyber versus terrorist attack. In the latter, public ownership and notoriety of who the perpetrator is, remains a distinct goal and desire of those perpetrating a terrorist attack. Also, while their methods of accomplishing the terror attack are usually simple and "low-tech," what matters to the terrorist is that the victims (as well as his competitors) know WHO committed the heinous act. By contrast, the cyber attacker prefers to be cloaked in secret, to act stealthily, not revealing highly-complex methods, sources, or signatures, while being able to suddenly and massively disrupt broad technological networks. As such, the proposed SAFETY Act amendment appropriately focuses on whether a qualifying cyber incident causes "material levels of damage" and "severely affects" the United States, as the "trigger" for coverage, not on whether the attacker can be labeled a "terrorist."

Second, over the past 13 years, pursuit of SAFETY Act coverage has become a "best practice" for companies in the homeland security market, which necessarily requires such companies to demonstrate "proven effectiveness" of their anti-terror products or services. Indeed, DHS already has awarded coverage for certain cybersecurity solutions and technologies. DHS's focus on "proven effectiveness" will apply equally to cyber solution providers and those companies that are deciding on the quality and scope of their cyber threat protections program. As such, the SAFETY Act should have the salutary benefit of improving the quality of cyber technology and use, thereby hardening networks and enhancing the level of cybersecurity generally throughout the United States.

Third, as a prerequisite to obtaining SAFETY Act protection, the Act has always required an applicant to maintain terror insurance coverage; the amendment would similarly require an applicant to maintain cyber insurance to obtain the protections. This combination of liability protections and insurance requirements spurred the terror insurance markets to open up and will likely have the same effect on cyber insurance markets, particularly in the highly-vulnerable aviation, health, electric, and energy critical infrastructure arenas. Similarly, if SAFETY Act liability protection is provided to those companies providing proven cyber solutions, especially to high-value targeted industries, the insurance markets will likely respond positively because of the layer of immunity and claims-elimination protection afforded to its insureds if they are sued after a "qualifying cyber incident."

Fourth, the procedures for obtaining SAFETY Act coverage have been demonstrated to be reasonably predictable and, when needed, nimble. These procedures include protocols for expediting or "fast-tracking" applications; modifying a coverage award when a company's technology has materially changed; and renewing coverage after an initial award. Companies who fail to update DHS with material changes to their technology or fail to provide the technology or service as outlined to DHS in obtaining SAFETY Act coverage could find themselves without protection should a lawsuit arise.

That said, the challenge for the SAFETY Act Office will be to obtain the necessary resources and expertise to handle an increased number of cyber-based SAFETY Act applications and to be able to nimbly but meaningfully review cyber applications which inherently involve changing technologies and threat environments.

Finally, the proposed legislation does not conflict with the Senate information-sharing and monitoring bills. These bills focus on the important need to enhance a specific critical activity—the sharing of cyber threat information between and among commercial and Governmental entities—by providing protection for such sharing and monitoring companies from liability arising out of these specific activities. The proposed House legislation is focused on those companies that design, develop, and deploy and use cyber solutions, e.g., threat and theft protection; vulnerability assessments; fraud and identity protection, etc. The House legislation is meant to incentivize a broad swath of providers and users of such cyber technology by providing significant tort protections afforded under the SAFETY Act should a "qualifying cyber incident" occur.

CONCLUSION

The proposed legislation to discriminately expand the SAFETY Act is reasonably calculated to address both policy-based concerns and market dynamics. Its emphasis on the severity and impact of the cyber attack and not on the identity of the attacker as the trigger for protection is appropriate. DHS's continued requirement that a technology—cyber or otherwise—have a record of "proven effectiveness" and the statutory requirement to carry cyber insurance, will likely spur higher quality technology and more available insurance. The challenge for the DHS SAFETY Act Office will be to have sufficient qualified resources who can conduct meaningful and timely reviews in an atmosphere of rapidly-changing technology and threats. In the end, this amendment, like the original SAFETY Act, should be driven by a common spirit and intent: To take proactive legislative incentivizing steps now—to avoid a catastrophic debilitating incident involving a major critical infrastructure or economic sector of the United States. This proposed discriminate amendment of the SAFETY Act is a step in the right direction.

Mrs. WATSON COLEMAN. Mr. Chairman.

Mr. RATCLIFFE. Thank you, Mr. Biagini.

The Chair now recognizes Mrs. Watson Coleman.

Mrs. WATSON COLEMAN. Thank you, Mr. Chairman, and thank you, Mr. Langevin.

I just want to take this opportunity to acknowledge and welcome and thank Dr. Andrea Matwyshyn for being here today and being a part of this very impressive panel.

Dr. Matwyshyn is currently the Microsoft visiting professor at the Center for Technology Policy at Princeton University, which is part of the 12th Congressional District that I am proud to serve.

She is a legal academic studying technology innovation and its legal implications, particularly corporate information. In 2013 to 2014, she served as a senior policy advisor and academic in residence at the U.S. Federal Trade Commission, focusing her work on corporate information security issues.

She is a full professor of law at Northeastern University and a faculty affiliate of the Center for Internet and Society of Stanford Law School. She has had many very impressive appointments at many very impressive schools, from the Wharton School, the University of Pennsylvania, all the way to the Singapore Management University, Cambridge University, University of Oxford, and Notre Dame.

Prior to entering academia, she was a private attorney, focusing her work on technology transactions. She has previously testified on issues of information security, and she is called upon and often quoted on these issues.

We are delighted to have her today, and thank you for having this hearing and providing this opportunity for us to hear from her.

Thank you.

With that, I yield back.

Mr. RATCLIFFE. The gentlelady yields back. I thank the gentlelady for that introduction, and also glad to have you as part of our subcommittee today. A number of the Democratic Members of this subcommittee are traveling with the President presently overseas, so we very much appreciate you being here with us today.

With that, the Chair recognizes Dr. Matwyshyn for 5 minutes for her opening statement.

**STATEMENT OF ANDREA M. MATWYSHYN, VISITING PRO-
FESSOR, CENTER FOR INFORMATION TECHNOLOGY POLICY,
PRINCETON UNIVERSITY**

Ms. MATWYSHYN. Thank you.

Chairman Ratcliffe, Member Langevin, and other distinguished
Members of the subcommittee, it is my great honor to be with you
here today to discuss the topic that I have devoted my academic
career to studying: Information security and the National crisis
that we face in working toward making our Nation more secure,
both in terms of our defense and in terms of our economy in particular.

The SAFETY Act was passed in 2002, and, at that time, it un-
doubtedly served as a critically-stimulating impetus for the emer-
gence of physical space products from entrepreneurs to enable our
society to move toward a more secure physical environment. However, the SAFETY Act in 2015 is, unfortunately, not an optimal fit
for the information security ecosystem.

The information security ecosystem is one that is driven by constant, frequently overnight, innovation. As such, expanding or in-
terpreting the SAFETY Act to provide liability limitation for product, certain products only, in the information security ecosystem
will disrupt rather than encourage an already successfully bur-
geoning market of cutting-edge information security products and
services.

The market is projected to reach approximately $93 billion worth
of information security products and services in the next 2 years.
We are seeing many successful IPOs; we are seeing venture cap-
italists investing heavily.

Expanding or including information security within the SAFETY
Act liability limitations will, in essence, negatively shift the purchasing behaviors of companies away from determining products
based on the recommendations of their information security engineers and code quality toward the recommendations of CFOs, general counsel, and other perhaps less technologically-sophisticated
individuals who are concerned about risk mitigation rather than information security first and foremost.

As such, the certification period is not a fit for information security technologies. Instead, it is likely to engender a false sense of
security in enterprises and may, unfortunately, incentivize them to,
for example, fail to comply with the new ISO standards in information security or to obtain the relevant information security policies
that the insurance industry increasingly offers, with over 50 major
insurance companies now having robust offerings set in this space.

The next few points I will briefly mention are elaborated upon
more thoroughly in my written testimony.

As I was preparing for this hearing, the availability of information regarding the transparency of the process of certification was,
in my opinion, not as thorough as I would have hoped to be able
to have an objective assessment of it. In particular, it is critical
that any certification that provides the substantial benefit of a limitation of liability be driven by an independent, rigorous, third-
party testing, including penetration testing and all the state-of-the-
art technology measures that would be best suited to this kind of
certification.

With DHS having, unfortunately, limited capability in enforcement, this means that companies may be unwilling to correct their technologies in a timely manner when DHS even finds a problem. In fact, we see this behavior from companies in the current marketplace.

So the expansion or inclusion of the SAFETY Act limited liability framework for information security products would, unfortunately, I believe, create disincentives to fix, timely patch, and well-disclose in security advisories the types of information that is absolutely critical to companies and to our agencies in defending us in a holistic approach with respect to the information security threats that we face.

Context is everything, and the only way that we will succeed in defending our Nation and our economy is through a multi-lateral, coordinated approach between the public sector and the private sector that is sensitive to this set of moving pieces that need to be coordinated simultaneously.

Finally, the expansion of this limited liability could impair the work of other agencies, including the FCC and the FTC. I have Federalism concerns, where the States, I believe, are the appropriate laboratories of experimentation first for any liability limitation approach.

Thank you.

[The prepared statement of Ms. Matwyshyn follows:]

PREPARED STATEMENT OF ANDREA M. MATWYSHYN

JULY 28, 2015

Chairman Ratcliffe, Ranking Member Richmond, Representative Langevin, and other distinguished Members of the committee, it is my honor to be here with you today to discuss the future of information security in the United States and the SAFETY Act. My testimony today reflects cumulative knowledge I have acquired during my last 16 years as both a corporate attorney and academic conducting research on the legal regulation of information security. My testimony also reflects the practical business knowledge I have obtained through long-standing relationships with insiders at Fortune 100 technology companies, technology entrepreneurs, consumer rights advocates, and independent information security professionals. Finally, this testimony is informed by insights acquired during my service as the Federal Trade Commission's Senior Policy Advisor/Academic in Residence, advising on matters of information security.

During the last decade, awareness of information security has dramatically increased in both the public and private sector, and State data security statutes have contributed significantly to this improvement. However, the field of information security is still in its early years, and the overall level of information security knowledge and care that currently exists in the United States is still inadequate. As high-profile data breaches such as the security failures of organizations such as OPM and Sony permeate the news, citizen confidence in the data stewardship capabilities of both companies and Government agencies is eroding. Dramatic information security improvements are necessary throughout both the public and private sector, and it is this social context that frames today's legal and policy conversation around the SAFETY Act.

The SAFETY Act's primary feature—a grant of limited liability to companies whose products are certified by the Department of Homeland Security and to their customers—is a poor fit for stimulating improvements and incentivizing adherence to best practices in information security. SAFETY Act certifications for information security products are not likely to lead to improved information security in either the public or private sector. Instead, such grants of limited liability for information security products and services are more likely to have the inverse effect. They are likely to unintentionally create incentives for lower quality in information security products and services, indirectly undermining National security and consumer protection advancement.

1. Limitations of liability are likely to disrupt information security innovation in the marketplace—an outcome that contradicts the goals of the SAFETY Act—and to create disincentives for corporate purchasing based on information security technical efficacy

The marketplace for information security products and services has dramatically evolved since the passage of the SAFETY Act. While the SAFETY Act's liability limitation incentives for creation of new information security products may have been helpful in 2002, in 2015 they are unnecessary. The market for information security is robust and has matured significantly: According to some estimates, sales of digital security products and services are likely to approach $80 billion worldwide in 2015 and rise to $93 billion in the next 2 years.[1] Information security company companies are successfully obtaining venture capital easily and engaging in IPOs,[2] and high-quality information security products are successfully appearing in the market. Because of this healthy market growth, any selective liability limitation incentives injected today by the SAFETY Act are likely to be undesirably disruptive and damagingly counterproductive to the successfully blooming market for information security products and services.

Because of the fast pace of innovation in information security, it is likely that the liability protection offered to certified products by the SAFETY Act will outlive the optimal technical efficacy of those certified products. Yet, any technology deployed during the period of designation is protected for the lifetime of designation. Indeed, the older a certified product becomes, the more outdated and potentially vulnerable it is likely to become, particularly because material changes may require DHS notification/refiling to maintain certification. Meanwhile, the SAFETY Act liability shield remains constant across time. Thus, it is precisely the older, potentially more vulnerable certified technologies that may command a lower pricepoint and superficially appear most cost-effective to corporate decision makers without technical expertise.

As a consequence, business purchasing incentives could undesirably shift away from maximizing best practices in information security in favor of maximizing liability limitation. Corporate CFOs and general counsels will be likely to override the technical judgement of the CISO and their information security engineers in at least a portion of corporate information security products purchasing decisions. Companies will therefore likely shift away from purchasing based primarily on technical efficacy toward purchasing information security products based on whether they are certified under the SAFETY Act, even when those certified products may be of inferior technical quality or a worse business fit. In granting limitations of liability to only certain information security companies under the SAFETY Act, DHS would unnecessarily manipulate an already-competitive information security marketplace, potentially hindering adoption of new information security technologies in favor of older ones.

A significant and growing portion of the information security expert community does not view the use of liability limitation approaches as the correct path to improving public and private-sector information security. As vulnerabilities will increasingly lead to potential loss of human life,[3] code quality and information security rigor in products become paramount. Similarly, sophisticated technology companies with heavy investments in information security in many cases do not necessarily support limitations of security liability, and they are concerned that less ethical companies are misrepresenting the quality of the security in their products and services. Due to low enforcement and lack of information security liability, the market currently inadequately sanctions misrepresentations of information security quality in products and services. Liability limitation for information security products will only exacerbate this code quality problem, unfairly disadvantaging the companies who purchase the best-of-breed information security products based on technical information security concerns and enterprise fit rather than based on DHS certification.

Selective liability limitation through the SAFETY Act also disadvantages information security start-ups. Start-ups are most likely to be allocating resources to code development at the expense of allocating budget to the legal resources necessary to apply for a certification under the SAFETY Act. Yet, security start-ups sometimes offer the most appropriate product for a particular information security corporate need from a technical perspective.

---

[1] *http://www.betaboston.com/news/2015/07/17/cybersecurity-firm-rapid7-raises-103m-in-years-first-boston-tech-ipo/.*

[2] Id.

[3] *http://www.wired.com/2015/07/jeep-hack-chrysler-recalls-1-4m-vehicles-bug-fix/.*

2. The level of technical rigor in procedures in the SAFETY Act certification process are suboptimally transparent

Pursuant to my review of available information regarding the SAFETY Act certification process, the process of certification is currently suboptimally transparent. Available DHS materials raise material concerns regarding the technical rigor and thoroughness of the vetting process for certification of information security products and services. DHS states in informational materials on its website regarding the certification process that it views itself as "nonregulatory" and that a body of un-identified "technical experts" will provide "suggestions." The process appears to be largely applicant self-reported with respect to product and services performance and quality. It is not clear from available DHS materials that DHS performs any inde-pendent penetration testing, analysis of code quality, assessment of patching speed or quality review of self-reporting through prior applicant security advisories during the process of evaluating applications. Members of the information security research community have also raised various concerns regarding the process.[4] For example, my consultations with private-sector vulnerability database experts have yielded po-tentially important unanswered questions regarding the quality of currently-cer-tified information security products' advisory release history.[5]

An applicant-driven, non-transparent process is not optimal for a Governmental process culminating in the substantial privilege of a grant of limited liability for harms resulting from information security inadequacy. When these process ambigu-ities are added to the sub-optimally precise definitions in the SAFETY Act regarding the classification of security incidents and the broad discretion afforded to DHS in interpretation, substantial concerns exist regarding the current structure of the cer-tification process.

3. Grants of limited liability for information security products are likely to negatively impact timely patching, code integrity vigilance, and the quality of advisory disclo-sures in certified information security products

DHS currently lacks adequate enforcement authority to require correction of cor-porate information security inadequacies or to stop companies from selling dan-gerously vulnerable products in the marketplace. In fact, as expressly stated with visible frustration in DHS advisories, companies feel at liberty to brazenly disregard DHS's demands for correction of even serious security vulnerabilities in their prod-ucts and services.[6] Adding a layer of liability protection under the SAFETY Act for information security products would only exacerbate this bigger DHS enforcement problem, creating additional incentives for certified companies to neglect or delay patching or updating of their products.

Removing risk of liability eliminates an important corporate incentive for timely patching, internal vigilance regarding code quality, and release of adequate security advisory notices. The primary information security challenge faced in the market-place today is policing the consistent quality of information security products and services in light of their increasing vulnerability across time. Deteriorating quality and unpatched information security products create a false sense of security and leave their users vulnerable to attack. The liability limitations of the SAFETY Act do nothing to improve the quality and integrity of information security products. In-stead, they potentially create perverse incentives for lower levels of product and services vigilance through a liability buffer for certified companies.

4. Grants of limited liability under the SAFETY Act for information security prod-ucts may indirectly disrupt information security enforcement work of other agencies, harming our economy and National security

DHS's selective certification of particular information security technologies and grants of liability limitation may hinder the work of other agencies working to im-prove information security. In particular, the work of the Federal Trade Commis-sion, Federal Communications Commission, Securities and Exchange Commission, and Consumer Financial Protection Bureau may be impacted. These and other agen-cies are currently expanding efforts to police the quality of information security and data stewardship offered by businesses to consumers and business partners. These agency efforts are still in their nascence in many cases, but ramping up swiftly. A limitation of liability would potentially meaningfully circumscribe these agencies' ef-ficacy in using fines or disgorgements to obtain redress for consumer, businesses, and National security harms arising from information security inadequacy. This is

---

[4] *http://www.csoonline.com/article/2918614/disaster-recovery/fireeye-offers-new-details-on-customer-liability-shields-under-the-safety-act.html.*

[5] Interview with content managers at OSVDB.

[6] *https://ics-cert.us-cert.gov/advisories/ICSA-14-084-01* ("Festo has decided not to resolve these vulnerabilities, placing critical infrastructure asset owners using this product at risk.")

an undesirable limitation on important work by other agencies aimed at improving information security in our economy.

5. Limiting States' rights to impose liability for corporate information security misconduct will further erode consumer trust and damage innovation in the United States

Information is only as secure as the weakest link in the chain of possession. Therefore, it is essential that the highest possible floor of information security be created across organizations in both the public and private sector. However, the field of information security law is very young, and best practices of conduct continue to evolve rapidly. As such, determining the best legal regime for addressing information security liability will require experimentation on the State level to arrive at an optimal legal framework. A broader social and scholarly conversation on information security policy is desperately needed, and it requires time to develop. At this juncture I believe strongly that it is dramatically premature and undesirable to Federally limit liability for information security misconduct demonstrating a lack of due care in any form, including through the SAFETY Act.

States have traditionally been the laboratories of experimentation for novel legal approaches to liability. The best course of action with respect to any consideration of limitation of liability is one exercising deference to Federalism concerns and States' regulatory interests in redressing the harms of their citizens for information security harms. Different States engage with consumer protection questions in different ways, and no National consensus currently exists with respect to the best course of action for information security liability. Federally imposing the model of the SAFETY Act liability limitations undesirably breaks with the Federalist tradition of deference to State liability determinations. It also disrupts the traditional deference of allowing State contract law to be the primary source of liability shifting determinations between contracting parties. Information security companies are usually represented by attorneys who may lack SAFETY Act expertise but who are amply capable of negotiating contractual limitations of liability with business partners, as are, in turn, the attorneys of the companies that rely on those information security. Contract and tort law are already beginning to adequately rise to the challenges presented by the information security marketplace, and Federal intervention into software liability limitation is not necessary and premature at this juncture.

Thus, I strongly urge this committee to exclude information security products and services from the SAFETY Act and avoid legal approaches driven by limitations of liability in information security. Selectively granted limitations of liability through the SAFETY Act will hinder innovation in information security and negatively disrupt the information security marketplace. They are also likely to indirectly damage National security and stifle consumer protection efforts of other agencies.

Instead, I urge this committee to engage with a number of untried and more promising approaches likely to stimulate wide-spread information security improvements in the private sector. One approach that holds significantly greater promise is the repurposing of SAFETY Act funding toward phased-out information security tax incentives across 10 years for small businesses and entrepreneurs. These tax benefits would offer incentives for enterprises that are operating on tight budgets to invest in information security education, hire security personnel, and purchase information security goods and services. A tax incentive approach does not suffer from the significant negative secondary consequences described above, and it offers a more immediate and direct impact on improving private-sector information security.

Mr. RATCLIFFE. Thank you, Dr. Matwyshyn.

The Chair now recognizes myself for 5 minutes for questions.

So I think, as I listen to the testimony of all three of you, where I found agreement is that you all believe that the SAFETY Act itself is working very well or as it was originally intended, and the SAFETY Act Office, likewise, is a very properly functioning part of DHS currently.

I think you would all probably also agree, as we all would, that we do need to incentivize the creation of cyber technologies to provide solutions and protections for what is a very obvious and public threat to our cybersecurity right now across this country.

Obviously, where I did hear disagreement was Dr. Matwyshyn, essentially, her testimony is—or your opinion, Doctor, as I understand it, is you don't think that the SAFETY Act or the SAFETY

Act Office is the best place for this and could be disruptive, I think as you said, to the information security ecosystem.

So let me start with Mr. Finch and Mr. Biagini and give you an opportunity to comment on that.

Mr. FINCH. Well, I would disagree for several reasons.

First of all, first, when it comes to cutting-edge technologies being introduced into the marketplace, I actually think that one of the critical problems that we see when it comes to information security is that too many companies, as well as the Federal Government, rely on outdated technologies for far too long.

A critical problem that I have seen on a regular basis, for instance, is that far too many organizations rely on outdated signature-based technologies, standard anti-virus technologies. Part of the reason that is, particularly in the private sector, is that companies are extremely concerned about liability when they switch technologies. If they switch from a proven technology to one that is, "advanced" or "experimental," they are concerned that they can face liability for making a "wrong decision," and that there would be allegations of negligence or failure to exercise due diligence.

The SAFETY Act would give a level of comfort that: (A) The product has been vetted, and, (B), that there is some measure of liability protection associated with its use.

The other point I would make is that, when you go through the SAFETY Act certification process—and I know Mr. Biagini is exceptionally familiar with this, as am I—it is one of the most rigorous processes that you will ever encounter when it comes to determining whether or not there is a rigorous quality control, quality analysis, and continuous improvement process in place. You will not receive SAFETY Act protections unless you have in place a rigorous program to ensure that your product continues to work once it is deployed and that you continue to match threats. It is not fire and forget.

In addition, when the Department grants you liability protections, it clearly defines the threats that the device will protect against and what the liability protections will protect against. So if you have a standard signature-based anti-virus program, it will not offer you protections against non-signature-based, polymorphic, heuristic, behavioral-based malware with constantly-changing software.

So simply having a SAFETY Act-approved anti-virus signature-based defense isn't going to protect you and is not going to be an incentive to not adopt new protections.

Mr. RATCLIFFE. Thank you, Mr. Finch.

Mr. Biagini.

Mr. BIAGINI. Yes, Mr. Chairman. Just a couple of additional points. I agree with what Mr. Finch said, and I would add, you know, the comment that there is lots of investment going on, money is pouring into this area and so forth, what will happen to all of that if and when there is a giant enterprise-threatening attack on a critical infrastructure and liability is massive and is spread around—deaths, injuries, business disruption, companies' very existence is threatened?

That is what we don't want to have happen. We have to take the natural next steps to evolve the SAFETY Act to move toward that full implementation and protect companies to keep that investment going, No. 1.

No. 2, as Mr. Finch mentioned and you mentioned, Mr. Chairman, at the beginning about the SAFETY Act process being an ongoing process once you get SAFETY Act coverage, absolutely correct, it is not a static situation.

You, as an applicant, once you get SAFETY Act coverage, if you are upgrading your technology, if you are changing your technology in any material way, you need to go to the SAFETY Act Office. They are open for business to take on any modifications. They will do it in real time. The modifications will occur. Your SAFETY Act coverage will be upgraded to cover the next versions of what you are making.

So it is a very on-going process that is well done at the SAFETY Act Office.

Mr. RATCLIFFE. Thank you, Mr. Biagini.

In your testimony, you emphasize that severity and impact, not the identity of the attacker, should be the operative consideration in triggering SAFETY Act protections.

Can you give a scenario of how coverage for a qualified cyber incident would be triggered? In answering that, would you comment on whether or not you think any of the cyber incidents that have occurred to date rise to that level of severity and impact?

Mr. BIAGINI. Well, certainly, I think an attack on the electrical grid of the United States, nuclear plants, our energy sources, our water treatment sectors, any attacks like that that would debilitate, take down our ability to deliver those kinds of absolute necessities to the American citizenry would constitute the kind of severely impactful incidents that would receive coverage under this amendment.

Do any of the ones that have occurred to date, in my mind, rise to that level? Possibly. Possibly.

But where I think the emphasis ought to be is on critical infrastructure—as I say, the health care system, the financial system, the energy systems, the water treatment systems, and so forth, those that make up the bread and butter, if you will, of keeping America and the populace well and safe. Attacks on those that cause great impact and material damage are the types of attacks I think should be recognized under this amendment.

Mr. RATCLIFFE. Thank you, Mr. Biagini.

My time has expired. The Chair now recognizes Mr. Langevin for 5 minutes.

Mr. LANGEVIN. Thank you, Mr. Chairman.

I again want to thank our witnesses for being here.

Mr. Finch, Mr. Biagini, it seems like you have kind of gone to the doomsday end of the spectrum on this conversation.

I guess I would like to ask Dr. Matwyshyn if you would respond and if you would clarify and give your perspective on that, on the SAFETY Act and liability protection, if that is the best way, as I touched base in my statement.

But, also, I would like to ask you, and then the panel can also chime in, does the information security expert community uniformly support—and I am asking Mr. Richmond's question, to clarify, on this second half. Does the information security expert community uniformly support the use of liability limitation approaches as the correct path to improving public and private-sector information security?

So we will start with you, Dr. Matwyshyn.

Ms. MATWYSHYN. It would be my pleasure to answer those questions.

Taking the doomsday scenario first and foremost, it would be devastatingly misguided in protecting our National security and our economy to allow the general counsel to be selecting the products that the security team is using in defending our Nation. When we are talking about that kind of a high-stakes situation, we need to have the security experts—the engineers, the chief information security officer—using the state-of-the-art technology, whether it is certified or not, to defend us and keep us all safe.

A technology at the end-of-life of certification is still certified. We could find ourselves with business decision makers implementing a 5-year-old not-fully-patched technology in critical infrastructure. That is not the optimal way to defend us against attack.

Information security changes dramatically, overnight in some instances. Think about Shellshock; it changed everything. A technology that hasn't patched for Shellshock 4 years later, that is a severe problem. That is not the way that we want to be making these decisions.

The liability doesn't exist yet. The case law hasn't developed. So the information security ecosystem is not being crippled by copious liability coming from all directions at them in the courts. So those concerns are premature.

What is not premature is the significant need to encourage companies to responsibly implement reasonable security practices through a holistic analysis of their own enterprise and to determine the state-of-the-art technologies that best fit their business needs, particularly in critical infrastructure.

Members of the information security research community do not support liability limitation approaches uniformly. In fact, many of them believe that the best security teams are being unfairly unrecognized for their efforts because of the weak enforcement of information security and that companies without the same degree of care in information security are getting the benefit of the marketing value of saying that they have top-notch information security when they actually don't.

So the top-tier information security professionals are not worried, in many cases, about the risk of liability at present, because the evolution of the product ecosystem would first recognize the bottom tier of sub-optimally secure product/services companies. That ferreting out would be a substantial benefit to the overall security of our ecosystem and the economy and our National security.

So the major changes that can happen overnight in security really require the use of the best technology as it exists in that moment, not one that is driven by a choice around liability limitation.

Mr. LANGEVIN. Thank you.

To Mr. Finch and Mr. Biagini, would you care to ask—could you give us your perspective on that part of the question Mr. Richmond wanted to ask? Does the information security expert community uniformity support the use of liability limitation approaches as the correct path to improving public and private-sector information security? To your knowledge, have concerns been raised by technology experts regarding this approach?

Mr. FINCH. Well, I obviously can't speak uniformly for the information security community, Mr. Langevin.

By the way, I very much support and thank you for all your efforts with respect to cybersecurity. You are truly one of the leaders in this community. You have done more to bring attention to this subject than, I think, most people in Congress, so thank you for that.

But I would say that the information security community is completely overwhelmed at this point with the number of threats. I think you would agree that it is really a triage matter for them at this point. Their problem is just being overwhelmed with the number of attacks and trying not to get fired when the incident occurs. It is not an "if" the incident occurs; it is not even "when." It is, how long has it been occurring? So it's very much, how do we get handle on this?

Part of the issue that is completely beyond their control is that they really can't do anything other than try and slow down the number of events that are occurring. There needs to be an offensive component of this, which is the responsibility of the other side of this dais. It's the Executive branch's responsibility, and that's a subject for another hearing.

But when it comes to liability protection, that's absolutely a concern of a number of the members of the information security community, because, remember, now the CIO and the CISO are getting a seat at the directors and officers table at this point, and risk management is coming to their plate. They are sitting in at the board meetings. They are sitting in at the stockholder meetings. They are learning about the serious concerns. They are being fired. They are being held accountable to the boards of directors and to the CEOs and the CFOs, et cetera.

So, absolutely, liability is of significant concern to them and how to manage that and, also, how to tell the difference between what is snake oil and what is not when it comes to information security technologies.

That's an important consideration when it comes to SAFETY Act, as well. Even if the liability protections are not triggered by a declaration from the Secretary of Homeland Security, whether an act of terrorism or a cyber incident, the mere fact that it has been reviewed by the Department of Homeland Security is extremely helpful to a CIO or a CISO.

Mr. LANGEVIN. Mr. Biagini.

Mr. BIAGINI. Yes, I would add one other concept. I think we have to be careful not to let the perfect get in the way of the good, if you will. The SAFETY Act process is a well-established one. The SAFETY Act Office has shown its ability to review and approve cybersecurity technologies.

There is great concern about liability in that sphere. It is on top of mind of many, many companies that I deal with. You know, the process that has been established over the last 13 years has been a good one; it continues to evolve. I think it can—I'm certain it can stand and meet and beat the requirements that might be upon it with this amendment.

So I would second Mr. Finch's remarks that liability is a driver here among the industry members. Even though there hasn't been a, if you will, debilitating attack yet leading to that kind of enterprise-threatening liability, what we don't want to do is wait for that to happen and then try to act with appropriate legislation.

Mr. LANGEVIN. Thank you, and yield back.

Mr. RATCLIFFE. The gentleman yields back.

The Chair now recognizes the former district attorney from New York, my colleague Mr. Donovan.

Mr. DONOVAN. Thank you, Mr. Chairman.

I will just open this up to the panel, because I am not sure who is the person who would want to answer this or who would have the expertise.

But don't companies protect their data? Don't nuclear regulatory power plants protect their systems, and the water treatment systems, without the incentive of having limited liability? Why do they need that incentive to do this, take these measures to protect themselves?

I open that up to anyone who would care to answer.

Or, if no one cares to answer——

Ms. MATWYSHYN. I am happy to.

Mr. BIAGINI. Would you like to?

Ms. MATWYSHYN. So I concur with the spirit of your question. We want our nuclear power plants and water treatment facilities to engage with the state-of-the-art of security for the purpose of protecting their operations and be driven by the desire to defend our Nation and our populace, not by concerns of limitations of liability and whether they're present or absent.

That's why the engineering determinations of the state-of-the-art security technology must take precedence, or we will inevitably see the data breaches that are permeating our society currently and the types of serious incidents that are, unfortunately, regularly happening continue and escalate.

The OPM breach, for example, that was much less the—if we look at the root causes, it was, yes, we have malicious actors on one side, but there were some basic, fundamental errors that could have been caught through a thorough internal audit and review process.

So we have standards, such as the ISO standards, now that will encourage companies and other organizations to perform these rigorous internal audits. We all need to learn and grow together to defend ourselves together as a country rather than look for ways to limit liability and just try to engage with reasonable standards of security.

The liability will, in my opinion, not emerge if companies simply engage with reasonable security measures. I trust our federalist structure of letting our courts across various States work with these issues and letting various States decide. No officer and director will ever be fired for conduct that reflects the state-of-the-art use of security practices. So the risk does not exist when companies engage with these issues in a rigorous technical manner.

Mr. DONOVAN. The other two gentlemen, Mr. Biagini or Mr. Finch.

Mr. FINCH. Yes. I think companies are very much invested in cybersecurity. I know that for a fact. Every director, every C suite member that I speak to is extremely concerned about cybersecurity. They know it's a problem; they know they need to do something about it.

Where they are held up, where they are paralyzed, frankly, is what do we do? They are hearing so much about, what is state-of-the-art, what is the best practice? Frankly, it changes depending on who you're talking to and what the news of the day is, with respect to a new vulnerability or a new attack.

Let's remember that our adversaries truly have the advantage when it comes to cyber attacks. To use military parlance, they have complete freedom of movement. They can pick the time, the place, and the manner of their attack, with absolutely no concern about being prosecuted or having their actions interfered with. There is no threat that a law enforcement agency—particularly if you're operating under the protection of a foreign government or in a lawless area, no law enforcement agency, no government is going to come after you and disrupt your planning. So you can take your time and practice until you get it right.

So, no matter how advanced your defense is, you will be penetrated. Breach after breach has demonstrated that. In a world where 500,000 pieces of malware are created on a daily basis, there is no way any company is going to be able to defend against that.

To the doctor's point, what is reasonable? That is the question. That is absolutely the question. I think what we're forgetting here is that it's not necessarily about whether there's going to be a liability, finding a liability; it's about getting to the point of when a determination is made regarding liability. It's going to be extraordinarily protracted and expensive in order to get to that point.

Litigation related to the 1993 World Trade Center bombing went on for over 15 years. Litigation related to the 2001 September 11 terrorist attacks went on for over a dozen years. Hundreds of millions of dollars were spent in legal fees.

Now, as two lawyers at the table, that sounds really nice, but, frankly, as an American, I don't want that to happen. I'd much rather see that we have companies investing in the right technologies to mitigate those events and likely stop those events or make sure that the losses are far less significant than they actually were on those two terrible days.

Mr. DONOVAN. My time has run out.

Mr. Biagini, if I could just ask you a second—a different question. Who determines what the best practices are? Is it DHS? Is it the industry that determines the best practices? If this amendment to the SAFETY Act is done, what is going to give those companies the protection under that limited liability? Who is going to make that determination?

Mr. BIAGINI. Congressman, a couple responses to that.

Oftentimes, when we file SAFETY Act applications, there are industry standards involved, there are regulatory standards involved, there are company standards and internal standards involved that are in play with an application. When the SAFETY Act Office gets an application like that, they look at all of those. They look to see that you're complying with, if not exceeding, the various standards that may apply.

In the situation with cybersecurity, I think we'll have something similar. We'll have regulatory standards. We'll probably have NIST guidelines. We'll have company standards. We'll have industry standards. The SAFETY Act Office will be looking at all of that, as they do with any application, to look for compliance and exceeding compliance.

Back to your initial question about, well, aren't companies already protecting themselves, what I do for a living is I defend against tort suits that are filed in court, and I represent companies that get sued. Oftentimes, when all they can show is they're complying with minimum standards, whether it's an industry standard or a regulatory standard, in court, that doesn't go very far. That won't get them a very good defense.

So, in order to incent them to go above and beyond whatever these minimum standards may be, whether they're industry or otherwise, I think that's why we're talking today about the possibility of the SAFETY Act providing those additional incentives.

Mr. DONOVAN. Thank you.

Mr. RATCLIFFE. The gentleman yields back.

The Chair now recognizes my friend from Pennsylvania, Mr. Perry.

Mr. PERRY. Thank you, Mr. Chairman.

Mr. Finch, I think, as has been noted in testimony, many companies are slow to make improvements to their management of cyber risk because security costs money, obviously.

How do you think amending the SAFETY Act to cover cybersecurity gives companies further incentives to adopt cyber best practices, if so?

Mr. FINCH. Well, first of all, utilizing SAFETY Act-approved technologies and services or going through the process actually helps contain costs, whether it's the risk-management cost associated with insurance—and, as Mr. Biagini noted as well, the actual improvement in processes, policies, and procedures, this is very much a best practices review internally as much as it is a liability review.

So you actually obtain efficiencies by going through this process and identifying problems that you have internally that are fixed going through the SAFETY Act process. They have to be fixed in order to obtain SAFETY Act protections. I have had any number of applicants say to me afterwards, "We're a better company for having gone through this process."

Mr. PERRY. But what's the cost? I mean, is there, like, a—is there some kind of way to measure the cost by either your revenues or your sales of your personnel or some way to measure the cost per increment to determine—I mean, at the end of the day, everybody's got to meet the bottom line, so——

Mr. FINCH. Absolutely. It's an individualized analysis. To be perfectly frank, there are a number of companies that elect not to go through the SAFETY Act process because they don't necessarily think that it is in their economic interest to do so, whether it's because their liability concerns aren't that significant or they don't have the dollars and they're satisfied just relying upon insurance.

But the companies that feel that their liability concerns are so great, they look at the potential expense of this process—which is free, by the way. It is a free process. The Department of Homeland Security doesn't charge anything. Where money is involved, it's internal personnel time involved in putting together an application. If you need to retain outside counsel or a consultant, you can have someone work with you in order to put that application together. That typically runs in the tens of thousands of dollars. When you amortize that over a 5-year period, it's not very much money for a company to go through that process.

But, at the end of the day, you know, you did hit on a very important point, which is that, you know, companies don't have unlimited amounts of money to spend on cybersecurity. They still have to operate a successful business. This is actually a very important point that we need to talk about, as well, which is that companies could spend as much money as they have in their treasury on cybersecurity products and services and best practices, and they will still get breached, and they will still face litigation after that breach for having negligent design or negligent implementation of their security program.

In all likelihood, that case will still go to a jury or to a decision by a court. Companies will say, well, what are we supposed to do in order to actually prove that we did the right thing? They may eventually be vindicated in court. I'm sure if someone like Mr. Biagini is representing them, they will come out just fine. But, again, they will wind up spending a lot of money on something like that.

So we want to avoid that kind of situation. We want to give them confidence and say, look, not only are you doing the right thing and spending your money wisely, but we'll also give you a little bit of limited liability protection, not a complete grant of immunity—that's not what this program is—but we will give you some liability protections.

One other thing I would like to say very quickly. I think that if you were to include cyber attacks and cybersecurity technologies as a small amendment to the SAFETY Act, one of most exciting opportunities that I see being utilized in this context is shifting the focus from cyber defenders to other companies involved in information technology.

When I was in 7th grade, I had a project in wood shop where we had to take an egg, and, using a few small pieces of paper and wood sticks, we had to build a crate around the egg and drop it from 5 feet and hope that the egg didn't break. Of course, I failed. I'm not very good at technical things, which is why I'm a lawyer. I'm also not good at math, full disclosure. But the point is that cybersecurity is like that brown paper around the egg. What's the underlying egg? It's the hardware and the software.

That hardware and software has lots of bugs and vulnerabilities. I think a wonderful application that is waiting out there is to have the underlying software and hardware developers go through the SAFETY Act process.

As Mr. Biagini knows—he talked about it with the airports, the port authority, et cetera—the infrastructure itself, not necessarily the defensive technologies, is now actually applying. Wouldn't it be great if Adobe Flash actually built security into its own product so we didn't have to design all these security products to stop it from having vulnerabilities that are exploited by the Chinese and the Russians?

Mr. PERRY. Thank you, Mr. Chairman. I yield.

Mr. RATCLIFFE. The gentleman yields back.

Because we have a number of questions that haven't been answered, the Chair will entertain a second round of questions. I recognize myself for 5 minutes.

So, Mr. Finch, to the points that you were just making with regard to litigation and limited liability and the costs associated with that, I guess I would like to hear a little bit about how the SAFETY Act Office currently works with insurance companies.

Then, separately, can you discuss how adding cyber incidents as a trigger to the SAFETY Act would potentially spur growth in the cyber insurance marketplace? You know, underwriters and actuaries grapple with risk analysis, and it would seem to me that this change would help with that, but I would like your perspective on that.

Mr. FINCH. Sure.

With respect to the SAFETY Act Office working with the insurance community, it works with a number of carriers as well as brokers to help determine what the marketplace is for insurance. Because, remember, under the SAFETY Act statute, there are actually statutory limitations as to the types of insurance or the amounts that the SAFETY Act can impose as a requirement on applicants. There are two. No. 1, an application cannot be forced to carry more insurance than is available on the world market. Second, an applicant cannot be forced to carry an amount of insurance that would unreasonably distort the price of their product, i.e., make them uncompetitive.

So the SAFETY Act Office has to stay somewhat in contact with the carrier and broker community in order to understand what the terrorism insurance marketplace will look like and will now also have to stay in contact with the cyber insurance marketplace to understand what that looks like.

Again, it is an interesting one, because the cyber insurance marketplace mostly relates to data breaches, at this point. It is actually a fairly limited marketplace, only about $3 billion in global capacity. The most insurance that any one company can obtain is maybe $200 million, $250 million for a data breach. Note what is missing: Physical damage, personal injury, loss, et cetera. That is not an insurance marketplace that is really available.

Having the SAFETY Act out there, having carriers know that they can sell this insurance but, with the SAFETY Act, they will actually be insuring products and services that they know have been vetted, will help them. It will help them collect data that will be useful for actuarial purposes and actually provide a more stable marketplace that will support their business model at the end of the day.

I would also add, too, that I was recently at an insurance conference, and it's a fairly obvious point but not one I had necessarily thought of—and, again, another failing of mine is sometimes I miss the very obvious things right in front of my face. But we as individuals do not carry one insurance policy for everything in our life. We have life insurance, we have disability insurance, we have health care insurance, we have automobile insurance, we have homeowners insurance, et cetera.

For some reason, we have been thinking about cybersecurity insurance as a one-policy-fits-all program. I don't think that is correct. I think there are multiple cyber insurance policies that need to be available.

I think the SAFETY Act would actually help stimulate that, whether it is my cyber HMO model, whether it is the reimbursement policies that we're currently taking about or some other types of cyber insurance programs that we haven't even thought about at this point. The problem is so broad and so significant that the SAFETY Act could help serve as a stimulus to really diversify the insurance marketplace.

Mr. RATCLIFFE. Mr. Biagini.

Mr. BIAGINI. Yeah, just a few comments on that.

Think about it in this sense. If an insured has these liability protections and they end up being a first line of defense should there be a cyber incident that results in lawsuits, the carrier is going to be more willing to sell insurance into that scenario, into that potential situation, if it already knows that the insured could defend itself in those lawsuits well with these kind of tort protections.

That is exactly what has happened when the SAFETY Act was passed initially, is it granted these presumption of dismissal protections, it capped liabilities, and so forth. That stimulated the insurance market back into action, along with the passage of TRIA. So I've seen a direct connection over the years in that sense.

Also, you know, when an applicant comes to the SAFETY Act Office and is trying to get SAFETY Act coverage and doesn't have insurance—terror insurance, in this case—the SAFETY Act Office will work with that applicant, will look for quotes in the insurance market that would be consistent with the revenues that this applicant is generating from this particular technology.

It is a very synergistic process whereby the SAFETY Act Office is being very responsive to that applicant. It is also pulsing insurance and getting insurance involved and ultimately writing insurance for that—having that applicant get a modicum of insurance in order to get the SAFETY Act coverage. So it is a very—there's a lot of synergy with the whole process of getting SAFETY Act coverage with the insurance industry.

Mr. RATCLIFFE. Thank you, Mr. Biagini.

Dr. Matwyshyn, as I read your testimony, your written testimony, it seemed to me that your perspective is that the liability limitation that would be granted through the SAFETY Act would be a disadvantage for cybersecurity start-ups.

It would seem to me that most folks would see a SAFETY Act designation or a certification that comes with the rigorous vetting that DHS would do—would see that as an advantage. So I want you to comment on how you see it as a disadvantage.

Ms. MATWYSHYN. I'd be happy to.

The first step in being able to file for the certification requires hiring a very expensive attorney. When two high-level information security engineers get together in a garage to start a start-up, they don't have that money. They are frequently the ones who are creating the state-of-the-art security products.

So we are disadvantaging their new, fledgling start-up, which may be the state-of-the-art technology and best capable to defend us and our infrastructure, in the purchasing decision of a corporate decision maker who looks at the choice of security technologies not solely through the lens of the technical rigor of a security engineer but perhaps primarily through the lens of liability limitation, broadly speaking, and other corporate concerns.

Getting the state-of-the-art technologies in place is the paramount goal, to the extent we can achieve it inside our economy and inside our infrastructure. So that's my concern with the entrepreneurship limitations that would result, I think, from an expansion of this act.

Mr. RATCLIFFE. Thank you, Dr. Matwyshyn.

Gentlemen, I want to give you—my time has expired, but I want to give you an opportunity to respond to what you just heard from Dr. Matwyshyn and that perspective that she has.

Mr. BIAGINI. Well, the doctor may be interested in knowing that, oftentimes, we take on clients that we don't bill and that have a technology that would make a difference in the marketplace. They need to be able to get it off the ground. They need to be able to sleep at night that, if they do sell it into the marketplace, they won't get sued out of existence if there is a terrorist attack or, in this case, a cyber incident.

Having SAFETY Act coverage has been the difference, many times, between that small company that decides to just sit on the sidelines and not do any further development and getting the coverage which gives them a boost in the marketplace, confidence to sell their technology into the marketplace without the fear of being sued out of existence. That has happened many times in my practice.

Mr. RATCLIFFE. As a follow-up to that, do you happen to know what percentage of SAFETY Act certifications right now go to small businesses?

Mr. BIAGINI. I would not. I would just be guessing.

Mr. FINCH. Mr. Chairman, I think that would actually be a question for the Office of SAFETY Act Implementation, which actually leads me to a point I'm rather remiss in not making earlier, which is that I do think what's been left out of this discussion is how well the Office of SAFETY Act Implementation operates. I would dare say that they are the best-functioning element within the Department of Homeland Security.

You know, we may have our disagreements with them at times, but I've always found them to be fair and reasonable. They are extremely dedicated to their work. To Dr. Matwyshyn's point, they are exceptionally helpful to small businesses and are very, in fact, proud of the fact that they will work with small businesses to help guide them through the process without the aid of counsel or a client.

It is, of course, a voluntary program. There is no obligation to retain an attorney. The clients that Mr. Biagini and I represent typically want to retain an attorney because this is fundamentally a legal process and the general counsel wants to have a counsel involved. But there are also plenty of companies that do this on their own. I know, in particular, that there are any number of small companies that have gone through this process and have done so quite successfully on their own, working with the SAFETY Act Office, which is dedicated not to approving applications just for the sake of approving them but helping applicants be successful.

Mr. RATCLIFFE. Thank you, Mr. Finch.

The Chair now recognizes Mr. Langevin for his questions.

Mr. LANGEVIN. Thank you, Mr. Chairman.

Before I begin, just to answer the Chairman's question, from CRS, in 2013, 60 technologies were approved under the SAFETY Act, including 22 from small businesses, that's 37 percent; 14 from medium-size businesses, that's 23 percent; and 24 from large businesses, or 40 percent.

So, if I could, I will go to Dr. Matwyshyn before I have a couple questions I'd like to ask.

This has obviously been a wide-ranging discussion today and great point-and-counterpoint, which is how I would like to debate. So I will ask if there is anything that really stands out that you would like to mention for the record. Then I have a couple questions.

Ms. MATWYSHYN. Yes, just a few points.

First and most fundamentally, the question of whether an enterprise is compromised or attacked goes to whether there are underlying vulnerabilities. So the first step in a strong information security program of any sort is the self-analysis to identify those vulnerabilities. Buying a product that has a certification will not address the underlying corporate information security problems that exist in various enterprises.

Also, those purchased products are frequently misimplemented. So having the in-house staff necessary to engage with the technical-rigor piece of this is absolutely essential.

But one historical fact that, if I may, I'd like to bring to our attention is that there is a robust evolution happening in contracting practices across various entities with respect to information security liability shifting. So we have private-sector, private-ordering solutions that are getting at some of these problems that we're talking about today. We just need to let the market work through some of these problems in private-ordering ways.

So some of the liability concerns, to the extent they exist, are being addressed contractually now. That's exactly what happened after September 11. I was a practicing corporate attorney at that time, and we modified our contracts. So there were new provisions that were incorporated as needed to shift liability to address some of these types of new risks that were emerging.

To the extent that the information security insurance market is emerging, it's my understanding that there is some granularity in the types of policies based on the types of enterprise that the particular insurance companies are targeting.

So I think the major point that I'd like to emphasize is that the underlying defensive posture of the vulnerable enterprises needs to be the focal point of any successful holistic information security improvement program and ensuring that they are fixing the challenges that they face, the problems that they have in terms of vulnerabilities in the code that's implemented inside their organizations, first and foremost. Then the secondary concerns of purchasing various products to assist them, that is a second-tier concern. The underlying problematic flaws that they may have in their enterprise is where we start, in terms of the approach.

The last point I'll just quickly mention. To that end, I think we have not yet tried certain other types of incentive programs, such as, for example, tax incentives to small businesses to encourage them to engage with education in information security, hire more information security staff, or to conduct meaningful self-audits and get auditors in.

So, personally, I think that tax incentives would be a stronger way to go to raise the bottom level of the floor of information security across our economy. So I'd submit that as a potential other avenue.

Mr. LANGEVIN. Sure. Thank you. I like that point, as well.

So, as a matter of fairness, I want to give both to Mr. Finch and Mr. Biagini the opportunity to say—to ask if there's anything in particular that you've been champing at the bit to clarify or add.

But before I could do that, if I could just ask this one question. Hopefully, we can do this very briefly. Following up on the Chairman's earlier question, I'd like to ask each of you specifically, is there a cyber incident since 2002 that you believe should be Classified under a definition of "cybersecurity incident"?

Mr. FINCH. Oh, there could be several. I think that the data breach at USIS theoretically could be a cyber incident. While that was targeted and only involved 250,000 or so records, that was conducted by a nation-state, and that was done purposefully for espionage purposes and to commit harm. It could cause all sorts of National security and other types of harm. So that, theoretically, could be a cyber incident.

If there was actual dollar losses associated with the distributed denial-of-service attacks by the Iranian Government and its cohorts against the banking industry, I believe it was about 2 years ago now, theoretically, that could be a cyber incident, as well.

We've been fortunate in that there's been no kinetic events that have occurred within the United States, but they have occurred. There's been gas pipeline explosions in Turkey. There has been destruction of furnaces in industrial plants in Germany, I believe it was. Those would certainly qualify as cyber incidents.

I also think, though, that, you know, we're fortunate in that, you know, I'm sort-of struggling a little bit to identify some particular cyber incidents. That shows that—one concern that I've heard is that this may be overused. It actually demonstrates that this is something that wouldn't necessarily be used that often. Much like there has been no declared act of terrorism because, knock on wood, we haven't truly had a significant act of terrorism on United States soil since 9/11.

In situations where we have had some, such as the Boston bombing or if you want to call the recent events in Chattanooga an act of terrorism, which, again, is beyond my purview, there really weren't any SAFETY Act-approved technologies or services in the area such that there was a need to designate the event an act of terrorism.

But I do feel confident in saying that, with the spread of advanced cyber attacks capabilities, it's coming. When you can go out on the Dark Web and buy malware for $30, when you can buy zero-days for a couple hundred dollars or maybe $1,000 or $2,000, and you can buy the services of hackers for less than the cost of getting one of my daughters to clean her room, which is not a lot of money—and, in my case, my daughters still don't do it—the point is that there will be some significant, significant events that will occur in the near future, and we will all, unfortunately, realize that we live in a very dangerous cyber era.

Mr. LANGEVIN. With the Chairman's indulgence, if you'd have any points that you are champing at the bit to clarify or add?

Mr. BIAGINI. No. Just that, prior to 9/11, I remember a number of companies doing a lot of investment in anti-terror devices and homeland security activity, and then 9/11 occurred, and all of a sudden there was things that dried up. The insurance dried up for terror coverage. Companies were not willing to do any more investment in R&D for homeland security technology. We had to stimulate that, and we did, through the SAFETY Act and TRIA and so forth.

I just don't want us to be in that situation, where we do nothing here, we say status quo; an attack occurs that we can all agree on is of the kind that we're talking about; and then we're standing here saying, why didn't we do something when we had a chance?

We have a chance to be proactive and to get out ahead of this and do the kinds of things that will stimulate and make sure that we are belt-and-suspendering all of this, as the doctor alluded to. I think this is one of the tools to do that.

Mr. LANGEVIN. Okay. Very good.

My time is way over. I will yield back.

But, if I could, Mr. Chairman, I know that Mr. Richmond had additional questions, and I have additional questions. If I could, without objection, I'd like to submit those for the record. If our witnesses would respond to those in writing, we'd be grateful.

Mr. RATCLIFFE. Absolutely.

The gentleman yields back.

I thank all of the witnesses here for your valuable testimony and the Members for all of their questions.

As Congressman Langevin said, some Members have additional questions, which we'll ask you to respond to in writing. Pursuant to committee rule 7(e), the hearing record will be held open for a period of 10 days.

Without objection, the subcommittee stands adjourned.

[Whereupon, at 3:45 p.m., the subcommittee was adjourned.]

○